NAZARETH
GOSPEL SITES

Locating Events in the Life of Jesus

View to Catholic Church of the Annunciation with conical dome, nestled in the historic village site of Nazareth.

Book 3: Guide Book Colour Edition

TREVOR HARRIS

Key-line Christian Research Pty Ltd

THE NAZARETH SERIES
Nazareth Gospel Sites - Locating Events in the Life of Jesus
Book 3: Guide Book Colour Edition
Revised 1st. Edition 2017
ISBN 978-0-9925506-4-6 (Print Colour soft cover)
National Library of Australia Cataloguing-in Publication entry
Dewey number 232.9

ISBN 978-0-9925506-5-3 (Print B&W soft cover)
ISBN 978-0-9925506-6-0 (ebook)

Copyright © 2017
Author Trevor E. Harris

Published by:
Key-line Christian Research Pty Ltd.
P.O. Box 3205. Norwood.
South Australia. 5067. Australia.

All rights reserved. No part of this book may be used or reproduced by any means, graphic, electronic, or mechanical, including photocopying, recording, taping or by any information storage retrieval system without the written permission of the publisher except in the case of the brief quotations embodied in critical articles and reviews as permitted under the Copyright Act.

Disclaimer: All coordinates given in this book are nominal *Google Earth* positions which are not quite as accurate as the *Global Positioning System* (GPS). All maps produced are for illustrative purposes only.
Google maps produced under the conditions of *"Google Maps"*. Data from Mapa GISrael ORION-ME. Historic base maps are from the *Palestine Exploration Fund* (PEF) Survey 1880, courtesy of the Israel Antiquities Authority (IAA).

Cover and book layout design by Anna Dimasi.
Illustrations by Trevor Harris, Meg Stephens and Andrew Blaney.
Front cover: Artwork by Margaret McEntee entitled "The Prophetic Cross-beam".

The New King James Version (NKJV) is used for all Bible quotes
unless stated otherwise in the text.
Copyright © 1982 by Thomas Nelson, Inc., Nashville TN, USA.
Used within the terms and conditions stated by the publisher.
All other credits are listed in the text.

CONTENTS

INTRODUCTION 2
    About this book   2
    Jesus of Nazareth   2
    The Light of Zebulun   3

DEFINING THE CITY OF NAZARETH 5
    The mystery site   5
    The Jewish city-polis   5
    Location maps   9

LOCATING EVENTS IN THE LIFE OF JESUS 10
    1. The urban centre of Nazareth – NC   11
    2. The hamlet of Nazareth – NV   16
    3. The prophetic site of Sarid – Z1   18
    4. The Catholic Church of the Annunciation – NV1   21
    5. Joseph's home workshop – NV2   26
    6. Joseph's first burial – NV3   28
    7. Mary's neighbour or relative? – NV5   30
    8. The first church in Nazareth – NV4   32
    9. Joseph's public workshop? – NC2   35
    10. The Nazareth synagogue – NC1   40
    11. The Nazareth execution locality – NC8   44
    12. The Transfiguration on Mt. Tabor – T1   49

APPENDICES 53
    A: Other sites of interest   53
    B: The history of two Nazareths   54
    C: How Nazareth became Yafia/Japhia   55
    D: A Catholic source for Nazareth sites   58
    E: Prophetic signposts of the Messiah   60

REFERENCE SECTION 61
    Glossary   61
    Alpha-numeric site codes
    (All sites are allocated a code for cross reference)   62
    Index   63
    Promotion: The Nazareth Series   65

INTRODUCTION

ABOUT THIS BOOK

"This book's relating of the biblical accounts to the sites of Nazareth that we know today is a welcome contribution. It gives support to the reliability of the Gospel texts".

Ray Pritz PhD, former Director, Bible Society in Israel.

"Visitors to Nazareth ask many questions on the Gospel accounts. This book gives interesting alternatives for consideration".

Amer Nicola Licensed Archaeological Guide, Nazareth.

"Trevor Harris provides challenging material that requires a re-think on the understanding of traditional Nazareth".

Dr Murray Adamthwaite PhD, historian, theologian.

"The information in this book will help pastors and teachers to illustrate the Gospel events in Nazareth. The reflections will help those keen to know more about the life of Jesus."

Rev. Frank Eames ThM, pastor and Bible College lecturer.

JESUS OF NAZARETH

Illus. 01 The three language inscriptions on the plaque of Jesus' cross.
Image source unknown.

> Now Pilate wrote a title and put it on the cross.
> And the writing was: JESUS OF NAZARETH, THE KING OF THE JEWS.
> Then many of the Jews read this title, for the place where Jesus was crucified was near the city; and it was written
> in Hebrew, Greek and Latin.   John 19:19–20

The plaque on Jesus' cross decreed by Roman Governor Pontius Pilate has aroused debate over the centuries. The first part has raised the question of the size and location of Nazareth described as a city in the gospel accounts. The second is the messianic title that was rejected by many of the Jews. This book explains the mystery of the city of Nazareth and its key sites associated with Jesus' life.

THE LIGHT OF ZEBULUN

> And leaving Nazareth, He came and dwelt in Capernaum, which is by the sea in the regions of Zebulun and Naphtali, that it might be fulfilled which was spoken by Isaiah the prophet, saying: "The Land of Zebulun and the land of Naphtali, By the way of the sea, beyond the Jordan, Galilee of the Gentiles: The people who sat in darkness have seen a great light, And upon those who sat in the region and shadow of death Light has dawned".
> Matthew 4:13-16

When consulting many modern Bible maps the tribal area of Zebulun is shown as a land-locked enclave centred on the Nazareth region. However the biblical references to Zebulun clearly indicate that the tribal boundaries are located near a "haven for ships". The tribal emblem of Zebulun is a ship. Both patriarch Jacob and prophet Moses made predictions about this tribe.

- "Zebulun shall dwell by the haven of the sea, He shall become a haven for ships, and his border shall adjoin Sidon" (Jacob in Genesis 49:13).
- "Rejoice, Zebulun, in your going out … for they shall partake of the abundance of the seas and the treasures hidden in the sand" (Moses in Deuteronomy 33:18-19).

A careful examination of the boundaries listed in Joshua 19:10–16 with the archaeological and topographical evidence can show that Zebulun corresponds to the historical and modern region known as the *'Lower Galilee'*. This was certainly the understanding of Jewish historian Josephus who wrote: "As for the Galilee which is called Lower, it extends in breadth from Tiberias to Zabulon, and the maritime places, Ptolemais [Akko], is its neighbour" (Wars 3.3.1:38).[1] The proposed identification of the boundary sites is given in Illus. 03. Important and relevant in this book is the location of Japhia (Z8).

Reflection: A prophetic region

The Zebulun reference indicates that its tribal areas with that of Naphtali were to be the location of a "great light" that was to be shone to a people in deep darkness. Matthew's Gospel clearly indicates this is the dawning of the Messiah's ministry in the Galilee. It marks the start of a new era of hope and the promise of an answer to the human dilemma of death as a result of sin.

---

1. Flavius, Josephus 1987, *The Works of Josephus*, New Updated Edition, Whiston, W. (trans.), Hendrickson Publishers Inc., Peabody, MA, USA. Josephus is dated from 37 to circa 100 AD.

ZEBULUN MAPS

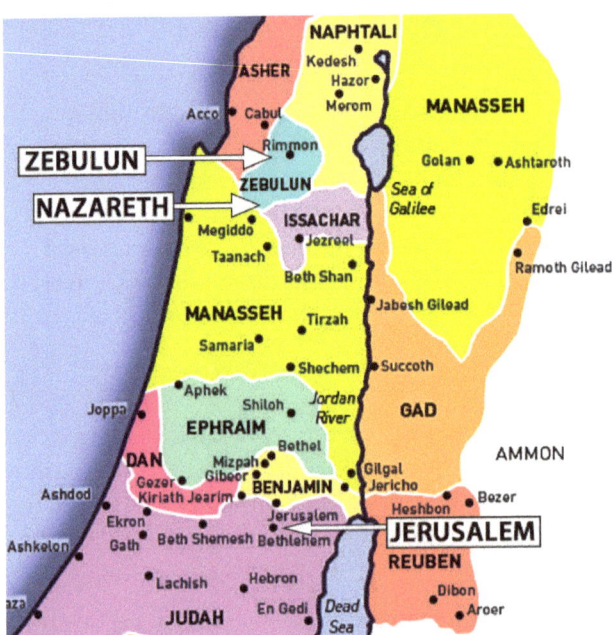

Illus. 02 The tribal map of Israel
Base map credit Mark Barry 2008.
Text boxes by author

Most modern maps of Zebulun show its location as a small land-locked enclave. This is due to several sites such as Japhia of Zebulun and Hammath of Naphtali being incorrectly nominated.

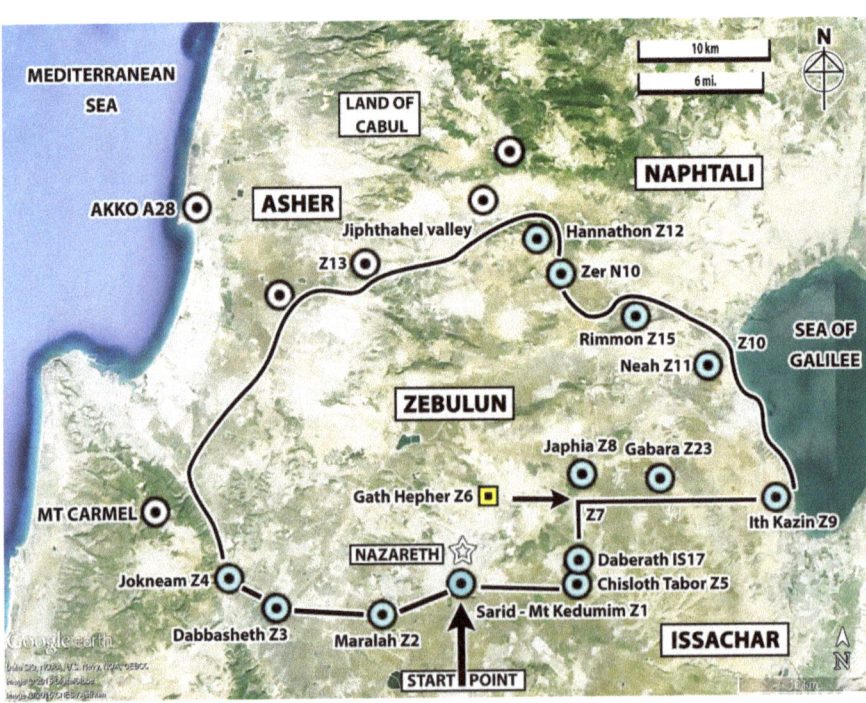

Illus. 03 Zebulun boundary sites based on Josephus and Joshua 19:10-14 explained in Reference Section p. 62. Base Map Google Earth. Image © 2016 Digital Globe.

DEFINING THE CITY OF NAZARETH

> And being warned by God in a dream, he [Joseph] turned aside into the region of the Galilee. And he came and dwelt in a city called Nazareth, that it might be fulfilled which was spoken, "He shall be called a Nazarene". Matthew 2:22-23.

THE MYSTERY SITE

> It is very doubtful whether the beautiful mountain village of Nazareth was really the dwelling place of Jesus. No such town as Nazareth is mentioned in the OT, in Josephus, or in the Talmud … Was Nazareth originally the name of a town (or village) at all? Encyclopedia Biblica 1899 [2]

The Gospels clearly state that Nazareth was a large city with a good-sized population. The current archaeological surveys in the traditional location do not support this. This has resulted in questions, similar to that quoted above, as to its existence and size at the time of Jesus. The mystery of Nazareth is solved when two important sites are identified:

- The hamlet that contained the residence of Mary and Joseph. This is the traditional location and the site visited by tourists from around the world.
- Tel Yafia which is proposed as the urban centre of the city of Nazareth in the time of Mary and Joseph. It is in a suburb of modern Nazareth located 2,500 metres (2,700 yards) to the south-west of the traditional location.

These two sites have the same name but quite different histories that are summarised in Appendix B. A detailed explanation of these two sites can be found in the publication *Proving Biblical Nazareth*.[3] A summary of how they relate in the Gospel accounts is given on page 10.

THE JEWISH CITY-POLIS

The Greek word used to define Nazareth is *polis* which means a large settlement with a high number of people and is distinct from a village (*'kome'* in Greek) or a hamlet. A Galilean polis was defined by three zones in 4 BC–30 AD (archaeologically part of the Early Roman Era 63 BC–135 AD).

- The walled city which was the central urban core having a secure perimeter with gates. It was often erected on a prominent, elevated location.
- The suburbs were adjacent to the walled section on the nearby slopes. They would provide support facilities and trades for the city.

---

[2] Reference: en.wikisource.org. (2016), *Encyclopaedia Biblica/Naphisi–Nebai*–Wikisource, the free online library, <en.wikisource.org/wiki/Encyclopaedia_Biblica/Naphisi–Nebai#NAZARETH>.

[3] Harris, T 2017, *Proving Biblical Nazareth*, Key-line Christian Research, Adelaide, South Australia.

- The outer perimeter contained hamlets and villages in a rural setting and included agricultural facilities. The perimeter was within convenient walking distance of the city centre.

Each city centre gave its name to the locality and this definition included the nearby rural zone. However, when Jewish cities were adjacent to each other there was a requirement to define the nominal boundary. The logical position would be the approximate halfway point between two city centres. There were three cities in close proximity to Nazareth:

1. Sepphoris, the well-known capital of Galilee and the headquarters of King Herod Antipas, located to the north (6 km, 3.7 miles).
2. Daburiya (Daberath), a well-documented historic city on the western side of Mount Tabor (8 km, 5 miles to the east).
3. Kitron or Cedron in the Septuagint, is proposed at the site of Tel Shimron to the west (6 km, 3.7 miles). (Shimron is incorrectly nominated)

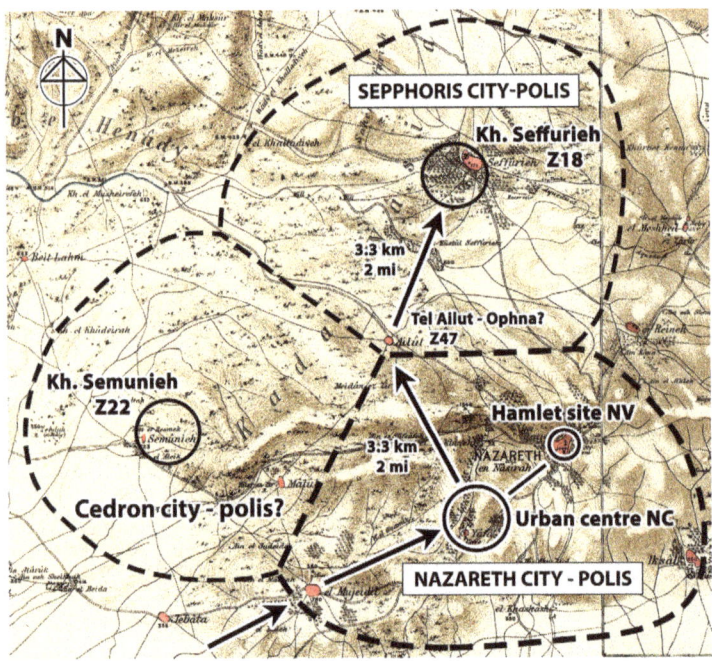

Illus. 04 Notional regional map 4 BC. Boundary limits of Nazareth city and the two adjoining cities. The arrows indicate the main road connections. PEF base map.

The spatial demarcation of Nazareth polis is important to understand. Archaeological surveys between Sepphoris and Nazareth have revealed a discernible cultural boundary between the two cities. The Nazareth side is distinctly Jewish in culture and the Sepphoris side is more multicultural.

Archaeologist Ken Dark noted from his surveys in the area:

"This along with other evidence strongly suggests that a Roman period cultural boundary existed between communities nearer Sepphoris and those nearer Nazareth." [4] Halving the above distances between the adjacent cities results in an estimated area of about 35-40 square kilometres (8,650-9,880 acres) for the polis of Nazareth.

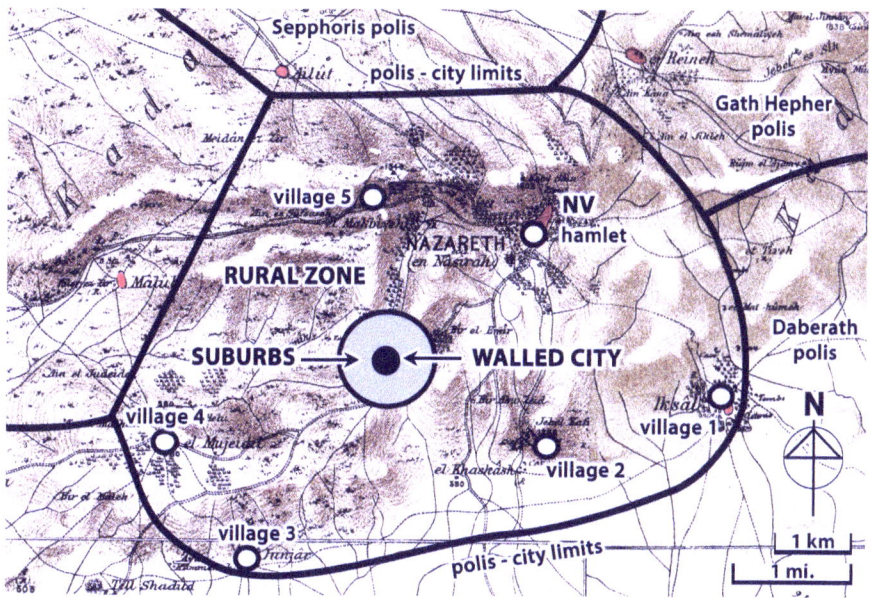

Illus. 05 Proposed boundary limits of Nazareth city in 4 BC showing the urban centre and rural zone adjacent. The hamlet of Joseph and Mary (NV) was included. PEF base map.

A critical definition

From the map above it is clear that the little hamlet where Mary and Joseph lived was within the city limits in the outer perimeter zone and not the central walled city. However, a citizen residing in the hamlet would still identify them-self as a resident of the city. The ancient Jewish understanding of the semi-rural perimeter was that its residents were part of the city. This was the case in the first century as described by Professor Ze'ev Safrai:

> Essentially, a polis can be defined as a self ruled settlement possessing the necessary institutions required of the polis ... During the Roman period *the polis ruled over the adjacent rural territory.* [italics added] [5]

---

4   Christianorigins.div.ed.ac.uk, CSCO 2016, *Dr. Ken Dark on Galilean Archaeology*, New College, University of Edinburgh. UK, <www.christianorigins.div.ed.ac.uk/2013/06/07/dr-ken-dark-on-galilean-archaeology/>.
5   Safrai, Z, 2003, *The Economy of Roman Palestine*, Routledge, London and New York, Section II. 4, p. 19.

This understanding continued into the following centuries and is proven in a quote from the Jerusalem Talmud: "And so it has been taught: Those which are near a city and are part of its landscape – lo, they are in its status". [6]

The map Illus. 05 is important as it illustrates the urban and regional spatial definition of the city of Nazareth. When this is understood the Gospel's city terminology can be understood.

The incorrect nomination of Tel Yafia

Unfortunately an error was created many centuries ago with the naming of Yafia in this location. This has robbed Jewish Nazareth city of its significance and led to a misunderstanding of events recorded in the Gospels. It has even resulted in some scholars proposing that Nazareth did not exist in the time of Jesus and that the Gospel writers were part of a conspiracy. [7] An explanation of how urban Nazareth was lost in time is given in Appendix C.

Reflection: A polis is correct

The Gospel terminology can be clearly shown as geographically reliable for supporting the traditional location of the house of Mary and Joseph.

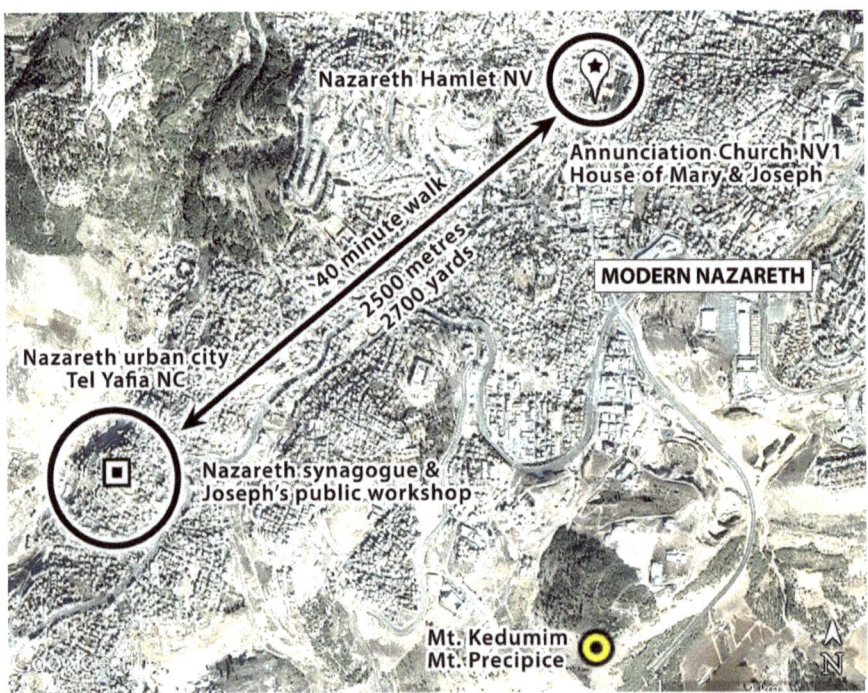

Illus. 06 The relationship of the original Nazareth city urban centre with the adjacent hamlet of Joseph and Mary. Base map Google Earth. Image © 2015 DigitalGlobe.

---

6 Talmud, Megillah, *The Talmud in the Land of Israel,* Chapter 1.1, IV.A Item C.
7 Salm, R 2008, *The Myth of Nazareth-The invented town of Jesus,* American Atheist Press, Cranford, New Jersey, USA,

Defining the City of Nazareth

LOCATION MAPS

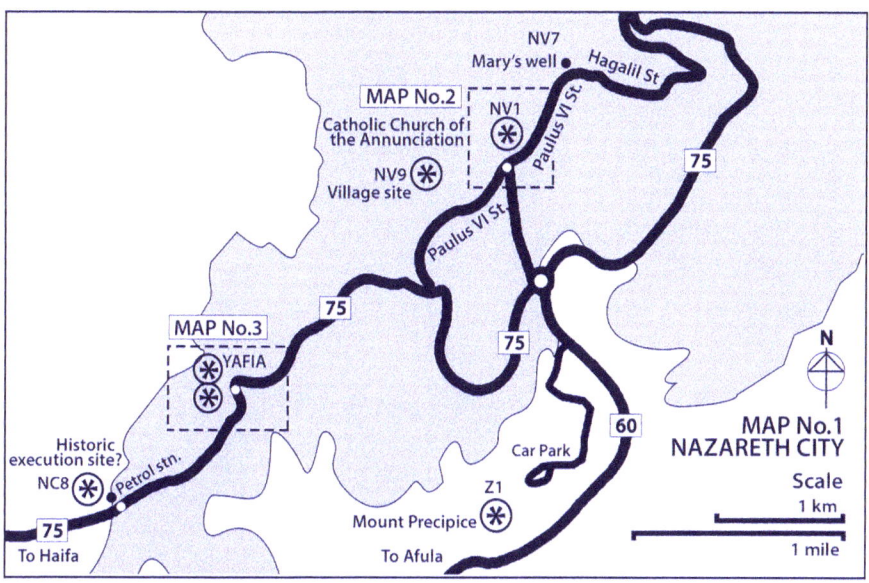

Illus. 07 **Map No. 1.** Nazareth City showing key sites in this book.

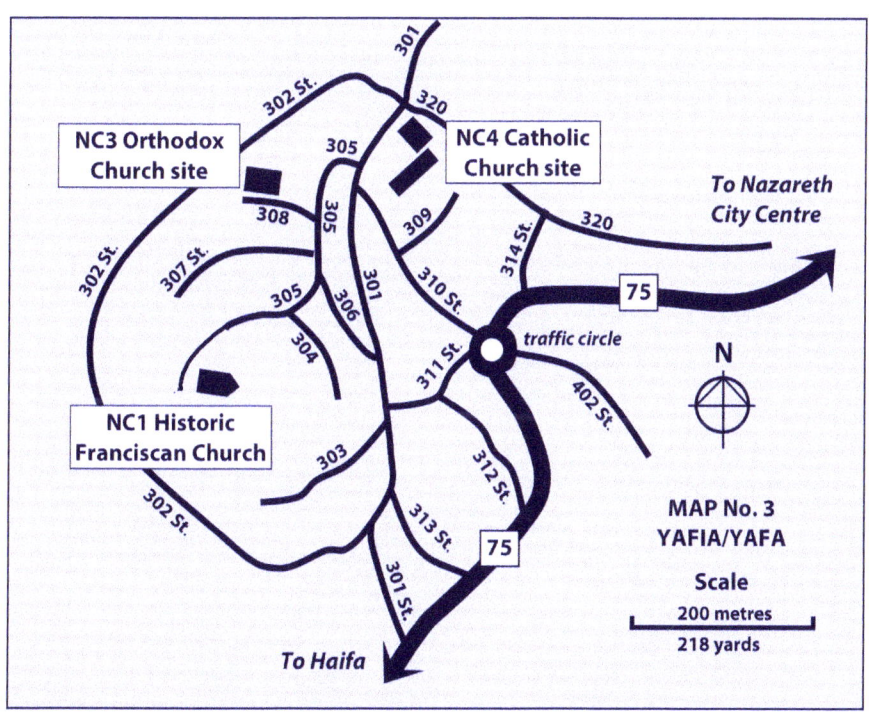

Illus. 08 **Map No. 3.** Locality map of Yafia (Yafa) a suburb of modern Nazareth.

LOCATING EVENTS IN THE LIFE OF JESUS

NAZARETH HAMLET – VILLAGE (NV)
A very small hamlet 4 BC. Traditional location of house of Mary and Joseph. Became a village after 30 AD.

2,500 metres – 2,700 yards
40 minute walk

NAZARETH CITY (NC)
URBAN CENTRE
(1st Century AD)
Currently named as Tel Yafia or Mar Yarkob

SITE NV
EVENTS RECORDED AT THE HOUSE OF MARY AND JOSEPH IN NAZARETH HAMLET

1. The Incarnation. Mary is chosen to be the mother of Jesus. The event occurs in a house (*Luke 1:26–38*).

2. Mary leaves her house to visit Elizabeth her cousin in Juttah in Judea (*Luke 1:39*).

3. Pregnant Mary returns to her house from Judea (*Luke 1:56*).

4. Joseph takes Mary as wife in her home in the hamlet (*Matthew 1:24–25*).

5. Joseph and Mary leave their home to travel to Bethlehem for the birth (*Luke 2:4*).

6. Joseph and Mary return to their home in Nazareth with baby Jesus (*Luke 2:39*).

7. After a short stay in their home, the Holy Family flees to Egypt (*Matthew 2:13–15*).

8. Joseph and Mary return from Egypt to their house at Nazareth (*Matthew 2:22–23*).

9. Jesus matures in the hamlet and city of Nazareth (*Luke 2:51–52*).

10. Joseph dies at his home and is buried somewhere nearby (implied).

11. Jesus travels from his home to be baptised by John the Baptist in the Jordan (*Mark 1:9*).

12. Jesus relocates with Mary early in his ministry from his Nazareth home to Capernaum (*Matthew 4:12–13*).

SITE NC
EVENTS RECORDED AT THE URBAN CITY OF NAZARETH

1. Joseph has a workshop/residence somewhere near the city of Nazareth (*Matthew 13:55*).

2. Jesus helps his father in the Nazareth city workshop (*Luke 2:51–52*).

3. Joseph and Mary had close (family) relatives in the city of Nazareth (*Matthew 13:55–56*).

4. Nazareth was a large Jewish city with leaders of questionable reputation (*John 1:45–46*).

5. Jesus taught in the city synagogue and was subsequently rejected (*Matthew 13:54–58*).

6. Jesus returned to the city synagogue to make his Jubilee Declaration (*Luke 4:16–22*).

7. Leaders pushed Jesus outside the city walls, towards an execution site on the ridge of the city (*Luke 4:28–30*).

1. THE URBAN CENTRE OF NAZARETH – NC

> Philip found Nathanael and said to him "We have found Him of whom Moses in the law, and also the prophets, wrote – Jesus of Nazareth, the son of Joseph." And Nathanael said to him,
> "Can anything good come out of Nazareth?"   John 1:45-46

- In a historic suburb of modern Nazareth spelt as Yafa, Yafia or Yafi'a.
- Archaeological evidence shows it was a large Jewish city. It was a civic and religious centre for an estimated 5,000 people in 4 BC–30 AD.
- The location of Mary and Joseph's synagogue.
- The place of Joseph's public workshop but not his family home.
- Incorrectly endorsed as Old Testament Japhia (Jafa, Yafa) by Edward Robinson in 1841 AD. Yafia is also the same as Japhia in Hebrew.
- Not all scholars have accepted this as the location of biblical Japhia.

Location: At historic Yafia southwest of traditional Nazareth by Route No. 75. Centred on 32°41'16" N. and 35°16'30" E.

Introduction

There was a northern migration of Jews from Judea after the success of the Maccabees in conquering Gentile Galilee in 101 BC. This included descendants of King David known as Nazarenes who founded a devout colony. They gave it the name of Nazareth based on the Hebrew meaning for a *branch* (Isaiah 1:1). It was a new city that started to develop some 80–90 years before the time of Jesus and therefore is not recorded in the Old Testament.

This settlement was located on the prominent hill of Tel Yafia which has confirmed city remains of the required Early Roman period. The Israel Antiquities Authority (IAA) has named the hill Mar Yarkob based on a medieval tradition that the sons of Zebedee, James (Yarkob) and John, lived there.

Nominating this site as Nazareth city will cause some reaction in archaeological circles because it is popularly known as the biblical city of Japhia.

- This was one of the border sites of Zebulun named by Joshua. His listing of the name requires it to be north of Mount Tabor. There is a location which meets this requirement known as Horbat Binit in Ilaniya north-west of Nazareth. Horbat is Hebrew for a 'ruined site'. (Site Z8 in Illus.03.)
- Scholars have nominated Tel Yafia as the 'Japha' of historian Josephus, who describes a fierce battle there between the Romans and the Jews in 67 AD. His descriptions can be used to show support for his fortification at Ha-Shomer in Ilaniya in the Galilee.

A Jewish city

The Israel Antiquities Authority has confirmed the evidence that this was a devout Jewish settlement. Their report states:

> The Late Hellenistic pottery reflects the renewed settlement at Yafia at the end of the second or the beginning of the first century BCE. [circa 110 to 90 BC]. The identification of the new settlers as Jews from Judea is supported by the similarity of some of the vessels to Judean pottery forms from the Hasmonean period ... This Jewish identity is further supported by the continuity of settlement into the early Roman period ... The chalk stone bowls and cups date to the Early Roman period and are characteristic of the Jewish population, reflecting a concern for ritual purity.[8]

This is crucial information as it shows the city was founded by devout Jews from Judea and extends into the time frame of Joseph and Mary. The IAA Report confirms the occupation in the required Hellenistic–Early Roman era. Nazareth as a city began to flower in this period and it expanded and developed to the size required for it to be called a polis by 4 BC. Being a good-sized Jewish city means that Nazareth provided a range of facilities for worship, education, commerce, industry and agriculture.

How big was Nazareth in the time of Jesus?

If the site was significant in size in 27 AD, the question is, how many people actually lived there? If this is answered it will shed light on events recorded in the Gospels. Yafia's historic *tel* (mound) is estimated as five hectares (thirteen acres) and would easily support 2,000 people within the urban area. The surrounding five villages with hamlets could house a further 3,000 (*refer Illus. 05*). This gives a total of about 5,000 which was quite large for a city at that time. This can be compared to the royal capital city of Sepphoris located to the north with an estimated 10–16,000 residents given by demographers.

The size of the congregation attending the central Nazareth synagogue can be calculated as about 1,300 worshippers.[9] This active religious community enables us to have a better understanding of gospel events, for example the large group of dissidents and leaders who are hostile to Jesus' preaching. It can show how he was missed by his parents in a large convoy, at age twelve, on a return trip from Passover in Jerusalem (Luke 2:43-47). It justifies the required client base to support Joseph's public city workshop.

A description of Nazareth city-polis

A Jewish city required a range of occupations and the Talmud listed desirable city residents to include charity workers, a circumciser, a surgeon, a notary, a slaughterer and a school-teacher. This gives insight into the cosmopolitan

---

8   Alexandre, Y 2012, 'Yafi'a', *Hadashot Arkheologiyot*, Israel Antiquities Authority Report.
9   Harris, TE, op cit. pp. 217–219. The demographics of the city and its main synagogue are given.

Locating events in the life of Jesus

nature of the city's residents. Based on the previous description of Galilean Jewish cities in the Early Roman period, along with Tel Yafia's archaeology and topography, a reconstruction of Nazareth polis can be made.

1. The walled city.

In larger sites the elevated section of a city was called the upper city, or in Greek terms an acropolis. The topography determined the wall position and for Yafia a preferred position with gates is shown below (*refer* also Appendix D.1). The protective wall would be the bare back of some dwellings as well as defensive walls with gates. This elevated urban form would have dense buildings with paved streets.

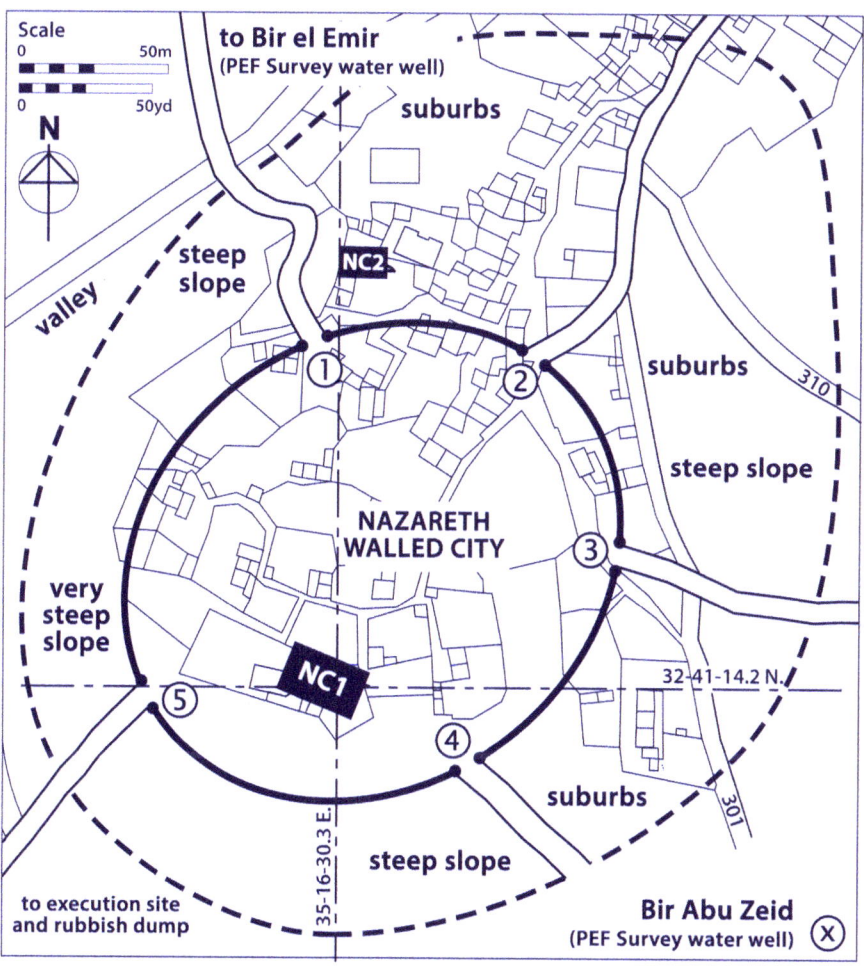

Illus. 09 Proposed upper city walls with gates numbered and suburbs dashed 27 AD. Base map by author is Yafia town plan 1951. *Refer* Illus. 33 caption. The Franciscan Church (NC1) and the Byzantine site (NC2) are sacred sites that are explained further.

13

This would be the city civic centre which included the main synagogue, religious administration and school for the district. There would be townhouses owned by the wealthy, the influential and the upper and middle classes, who may also have had villas in the surrounding hills. Courtyard houses of one or two storeys and compact row-houses would face directly onto the streets. Large underground storage silos involving three levels have been found in Yafia excavations showing first century buildings of some wealth.

2. The suburbs.

These dwellings were outside the city walls on the slopes of the main hill and in the adjacent valleys. The suburbs would provide support facilities and include the poorer and working class residents. Convenience and craft shops would be located near the city gates. Here would be the workshops for trades that were deemed to be dirty or noisy, as well as food processing places like bakeries requiring wood piles and ovens. Butcher and leather-worker shops would also be in popular demand. On the edge of the suburbs would be an inn for travellers and merchants. They would require facilities for the care and feeding of animals.

3. The outer perimeter.

This would have been the previously mentioned rural zone. Sheep, cattle and goats corralled with their shepherds would reside in this sector. Poultry would also be included, providing food and eggs. There would be olive groves and vineyards and the required presses to process their produce. Roman era remains of agricultural terraces, field towers, farmhouses and quarries for building stone have been found near Yafia and traditional Nazareth.

Illus. 10 View of Tel Yafia hill facing North. NC1 indicates the prominent location of the Franciscan Church, the proposed locality of the Nazareth Synagogue in No. 10.

Locating events in the life of Jesus

Illus. 11 View of Tel Yafia facing east towards Mt. Precipice (Kedumim) and Mt. Tabor. The hill was once the urban centre of Nazareth city with its city walls. The Franciscan Church (NC1) and the Byzantine site (NC2) are key site locations. Base Map Google Earth Image © 2016 DigitalGlobe.

The city water supply.

This is crucial for the settlement, and houses would collect rainwater from their flat roofs and then store it in cisterns. The IAA has identified a good source at a spring north of the city at Ein Sufsafa. Other springs and wells are likely to have existed in the floor of adjacent valleys (wadis) in earlier times.

Reflection: A significant city

Nazareth was a large cosmopolitan city in 30 AD. "Jesus of Nazareth" was the name spoken by many people. As well as Jesus' followers, it was stated by the Jewish and Roman authorities. It was even used by Jesus when he introduced himself to the apostle Paul in a vision on the road to Damascus (Acts 22:8). When Governor Pilate placed it on the title-plate (titulus) of Jesus' cross he specifically and legally described him from a known city. Nazareth polis was not an insignificant impoverished hamlet as supposed by many scholars.

2. THE HAMLET–VILLAGE IN NAZARETH – NV)

- The Catholic Church of the Annunciation is the most likely location for the event involving Mary and the angel Gabriel.
- This Church can also be proposed as the locality of the house of Mary and Joseph in a Jewish hamlet in 4 BC before it grew to a village.
- The site is a 30–40 minute walk to the nearby urban city of Nazareth. It was outside the urban centre, but within the geographical city limit.
- The hamlet site grew over the centuries due to extensive pilgrimage.
- It became known as the City of Nazareth after the original city centre nearby at Yafia was destroyed circa 630 AD.

Location: Nazareth hamlet centred on 32°42'7.5" N. and 35°17'50" E.

The archaeology to date does not support the Church of the Annunciation as part of a large Jewish city from 4 BC to 30 AD. The adjacent locality remains from the Early Roman era are very minimal in the first century and show it was part of a fairly isolated rural hamlet. However it did contain the house of Mary and Joseph and the distance between their house and the urban centre was more than a Sabbath day's distance of approximately 890 metres (972 yards). To observe the Sabbath and attend the synagogue they would be required to travel to the urban centre before sunset, stay with relatives, and make the return journey after the next sunset.

After 30 AD this locality was occupied by Judeo-Christians who later are also known by other names including Desposyni (relatives of Jesus), Nazarenes and Hebrew Christians. During the first three centuries, when Christians were persecuted, this site remained small. With the growth of Byzantine Christianity from 313 AD onwards, and the arrival of pilgrims over the succeeding centuries, the settlement became a village. The Christian scholar Jerome on his visit in 385 AD described it as a "small village". Eventually it grew to be a flourishing town and in Crusader times it hosted a large community. In modern times, this locality has boomed with the influx of visitors and pilgrims from all over the world, estimated in some years at over one million people.

Reflection: A prepared location

God did not intend that the special incarnation event was to occur in the middle of a walled city. It was to be a locality that was probably prayed over by visiting prophets such as Elijah and Malachi in the course of their ministries. The same Holy Spirit involved in the incarnation would have led them to pray for the future coming of the Messiah. Mary's parents were devout Jews so they would also have prayed for guidance for the future location of their daughter's residence.

Locating events in the life of Jesus

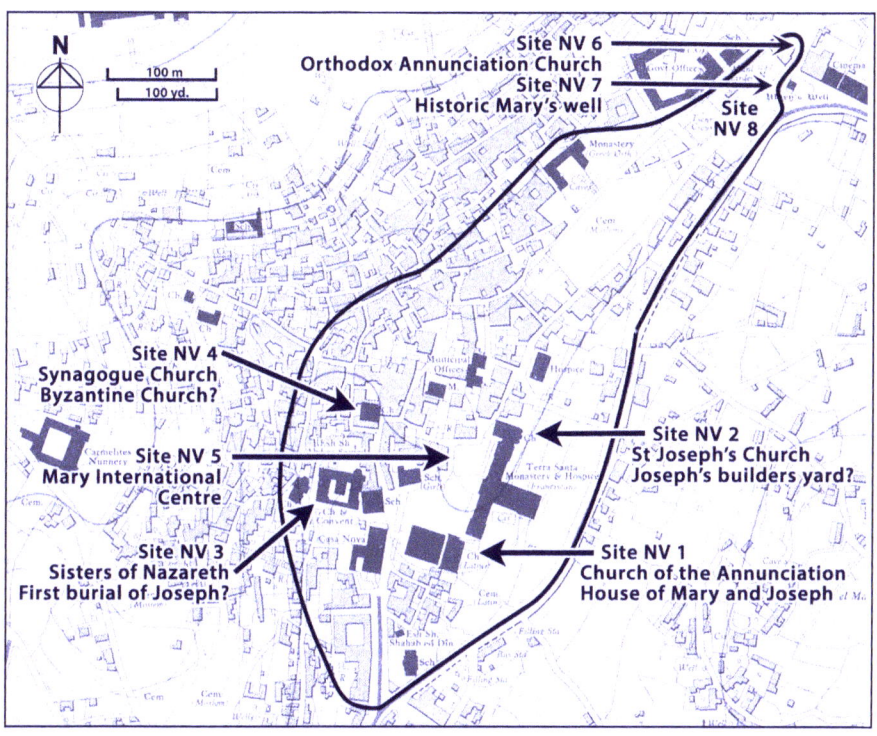

Illus. 12 Early Nazareth Village outline defined by archaeologist B. Bagatti Survey. Site labels by author. Base map courtesy of the National Library of Australia.

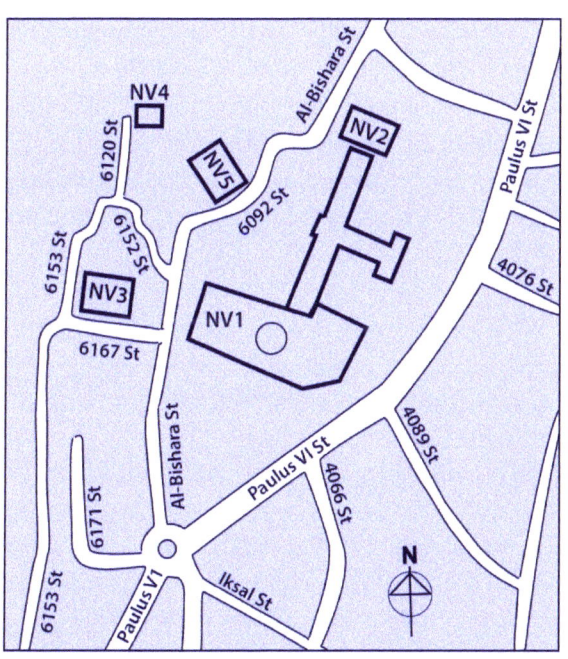

Illus. 13. **Map No. 2.** Nazareth hamlet locations. Refer Map No.1 on page 9. NV1: The house of Mary and Joseph.
Their adjacent gardens, builder's yard and stable were part of a very dispersed rural settlement in 4 BC. Later it was the focus of a small Judeo-Christian community (explained in No. 8) which grew as a result of pilgrimage after the fourth century.

17

3. THE PROPHETIC MOUNTAIN OF SARID – Z1

> And the third lot came out for the children of Zebulun according to their families, and the border of their inheritance was as far as Sarid. Their border went towards the west and to Maralah, went to Dabbasheth and extended along the brook that is east of Jokneam. Then from Sarid it went eastward towards the sunrise along the border of Chisloth Tabor, and out toward Daberath, bypassing Japhia.
> Joshua 19:10-12

Introduction

The key point to note is that Sarid is described as a set-out marker. Is there a reason why this was done for Zebulun's border? If Jesus was the promised Messiah it would be logical to expect some clues to be found in prophecies about him. Scholars have pointed out that Nazareth is not recorded in the Old Testament. However there is a clue in a spectacular mountain that lies due south of traditional Nazareth. It is known today as Mount Kedumim or more popularly to pilgrims and visitors as Mount Precipice. This is due to a Medieval legend that this steep promontory was the location of the attempt to execute Jesus by pushing him off a cliff .(This is shown as not the execution site in No. 11.)

Mt. Precipice - Mt. Kedumim

Location: Southern promontory at 32°40'50" N. and 35°17'52.6" E.

Access: Road No. 60 south from central Nazareth. Sign on the right points to Mount Precipice and leads to a car park near the summit. Map No. 1. p. 9.

This prominent geographical feature is a prophetic pointer to the coming of the Messiah. It is revealed when visiting the peak today. Although it is not the highest part, it is the most southerly peak and by far the most visually identifiable location. An olive tree has been planted in the centre of the plaza as a defining marker. This tree is a prophetic pointer as it is located on the same longitude as the Catholic Church of the Annunciation (*refer* Illus. 16).

- There is a cave in this hill with evidence of very ancient Neanderthal occupation. It is one of the oldest sites of habitation in Israel.
- Sarid is not a city but a geographical marker that is denoted on page 62. This is relevant criteria to understand biblical Sarid.
- In May 2009 Pope Benedict XVI called a large assembly of about 40,000 Catholics to a celebration on the northern slopes of Mount Kedumim. The theme of this special convocation was "Nazareth–it all began here". Catholics honour the event of the incarnation and it was interesting that they chose a location pointing north to their traditional location.

Locating events in the life of Jesus

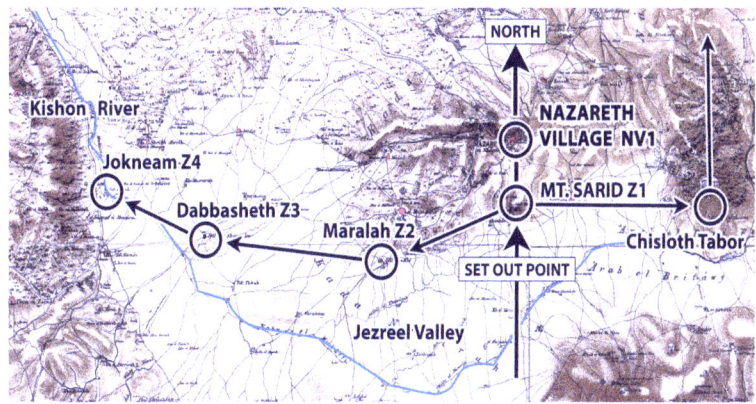

Illus. 14 The set-out point of Sarid showing the boundary definition to the west and east. This position points due north to the house of Mary and Joseph. PEF Base map.

Illus. 15 Mt. Precipice from the west showing the peak profile. The set-out point (Z1) arrowed is the olive tree on the south promontory. Credit: Almog Wikimedia Commons.

Three prophetic themes can be noted with the name of this peak:
1. Sarid means 'remnant' or 'survivor' in the Hebrew. One Bible dictionary notes it as "something left over, especially the righteous people of God after divine judgement". It further explained:

> The remnant passages are closely tied with the future king, the Messiah, who would be the majestic ruler of those who seek his mercies ... in that future there would be a new people, a new community, a new nation, and a strong faith in one God. This remnant would be personified in the Suffering Servant (Isaiah 53:1-12). [10]

2. Zebulun was the chosen tribal area for the Messiah to dwell for most of his life. When Zebulun was born, his mother Leah exclaimed after his birth:

"God has endowed me with a good endowment, now my husband will dwell with me" (Genesis 30:20). Zabal, the verb of Zebulun, is also used of God's dwelling in the Jerusalem temple by his Spirit (2 Chronicles 6:2).

---

[10] 'Remnant', *Holman Bible Dictionary,* Available at: http://wwwstudylight.org/dictionaries/hbd/.

Leah made a very prophetic exclamation at the birth of Zebulun. In his tribal region there would be the future honoured place of habitation for the Messiah. Mount Sarid is the set-out border marker and a prophetic signpost.

3. The prophet Isaiah on meeting King Ahaz in Jerusalem made the dramatic Immanuel pronouncement that "the virgin shall conceive and bear a son" (Isaiah 7:14). St. Matthew takes this event as prophetic and relates it to the Virgin Mary (Matthew 1:23):

"Behold the virgin (Gk. *Parthenos*) shall be with child, and bear a Son, and they shall call His name Immanuel, which is translated, "God with us".

Joseph and Mary can be described as belonging to the faithful Remnant. Their ancestors were part of the return of the exiles from Babylon.

The Mount of the Remnant points to the location where the conception of the Messiah occurs with the Virgin Mary.

Illus. 16 The prophetic olive tree on the southern promontory of Mt. Precipice (Z1) aligns north with the house of Mary and Joseph (NV1) indicated with the arrow.

Reflection: A devotional site

Mount Kedumim or Precipice is not the site of the attempt to execute Jesus. Rather it is prophetic Mount Sarid which means the site of the Remnant. It is the set-out point for the tribe of Zebulun and shares the same longitude with the proposed House of Mary and Joseph. The family may have had picnics there on occasions with friends and relatives. Jesus would have been well acquainted with the hill in his youth being a short thirty minute walk from his home. It would be a good devotional location with its spectacular views. He may have prayed there, reflecting on his future mission. This site is also a good candidate as a preaching place of the prophets such as Elijah, Nahum and Malachi. Jesus may also have preached there on occasions (*refer* Appendix D.9). Today, Christian groups use the mountain as a place to gather and pray. Mount Sarid should be promoted and understood as a site pointing to the first coming of the Messiah.

4. THE CATHOLIC CHURCH OF THE ANNUNCIATION – NV1

Illus. 17
"The Annunciation",
by Gustave Dore.
Courtesy of Pitts
Theological Library,
Candler School of
Theology, Emory
University, USA.

Luke 1:26-38

Now in the sixth month the angel Gabriel was sent by God to a city of Galilee named Nazareth, to a virgin betrothed to a man whose name was Joseph, of the house of David. The virgin's name was Mary. And having come in, the angel said to her, "Rejoice, highly favored one, the Lord is with you; blessed are you among women!

But when she saw him, she was troubled at this saying, and considered what manner of greeting this was. Then the angel said to her, "Do not be afraid, Mary, for you have found favor with God. And behold you will conceive in your womb and bring forth a Son, and shall call His name Jesus. He will be great, and will be called the Son of the Highest; and the Lord God will give Him the throne of His father David. And He will reign over the house of Jacob forever, and of His kingdom there will be no end."

Then Mary said to the angel, "How can this be, since I do not know a man?" And the angel answered and said to her, "The Holy Spirit will come upon you, and the power of the Highest will overshadow you; therefore, also, that Holy One who is to be born will be called the Son of God. Now indeed, Elizabeth your relative has also conceived a son in her old age; and this is now the sixth month for her who was called barren. For with God nothing will be impossible. Then Mary said, "Behold the maidservant of the Lord! Let it be to me according to your word." And the angel departed from her.

The Catholic Church of the Annunciation – NV1

Location: A prominent landmark in the centre of traditional Nazareth off Al-Bishara Street at 32°42'7.4" N. and 35°17'52.6" E. Map No. 2. p.17.

The previous text would have been verbally given to Luke by Mary when he was doing his research on his Gospel. The home of the Virgin Mary is the location for the announcement of Gabriel, also known as the Annunciation. The reference "and having come in" (verse 28) implies her residence at that time. The Incarnation (where the divine takes human form) occurs shortly after with Mary's full consent and cooperation. Being a devout Jew she would have prayed for the coming of the Messiah. Her surprise was more to her being chosen by God and the appearance of an angel. The virgin conception (verse 31) and the divine title (verse 33) propose this Jesus to be the Messiah. This location would be a very significant site in the salvation plan of God.

The Gospels note that Joseph and Mary were betrothed, but not cohabiting at that time. Mary was a teenager and still a virgin. Joseph was from Bethlehem in Judea and tradition suggests he was not a wealthy man. One explanation for the place of the annunciation is the home of Mary's parents named as Anne and Heli (or Eliachim = Joachim). Another logical explanation, supported in this book, is that this residence was provided by Mary's parents to become the family home of Mary. This was a common cultural practice of that time. A betrothed virgin would not occupy that residence on her own so it is highly likely that Mary's mother and probably a domestic helper were resident at the time of the angel's visit. They would be witnesses to the event (*refer* Appendix D.2). Joseph would most likely be resident at his public workshop site in the urban part of the city which is explained further in No. 9.

The archaeology

Mary and Joseph were resident from 4 BC to about 25 AD, except for their sojourn in Egypt for about eight years. Joseph appears to have died just before Jesus' baptism in the Jordan in 26 AD.

This gives a thirty year ownership window which is relatively small in archaeological terms. We do not know the size of the residence and no clearly identified remains of the original walls have been found. However there is good evidence of the site being occupied in the required archaeological time frame. The IAA report states:

"Many storage pits and cisterns, some which date to the Early Roman period, were found in the compound of the Church of the Annunciation". [11]

---

11 Antiquities.org.il. 2016, Israel Antiquities Authority, <www.antiquities.org.il/article_eng.aspx?sec_id=25&subj_id=240&id=1638>.

Illus. 18 Front entrance of the Catholic Church of the Annunciation. Located in the centre of traditional Nazareth.

Illus. 19 View of the communion altar table and grotto in the Catholic Church of the Annunciation.

After the relocation of Mary and Jesus in 27 AD the house would be seen as a sacred precinct and therefore a discrete place of devotion. Jesus' relatives would have taken ongoing responsibility as caretakers for the required preservation. An important point, not always understood, is that Mary's house was a unique residence. She knew its significance and only trusted Christians would have gained entry in the early decades after her vacating the site.

A history of the site

After the Apostolic Age (30-100AD) this site has relics of particular attention. The Franciscans claim they have evidence that shows the earliest venerated structure associated with the site dates back to a Judeo-Christian synagogue in the second century. Their website gives examples including a baptismal basin, mosaics and agricultural facilities along with pilgrim graffiti associated with it.[12]

---

12 Briand, J 1994, *The Judeo-Christian Church of Nazareth,* Franciscan Printing Press, Jerusalem. p. 23. My proposal is that Mary's room was located at the position of the current open altar under the dome, not the traditional site of the grotto cave some metres to the north. This location places it within the enclosure of the Byzantine Church as described by the Piacenza Pilgrim in 570 AD.

Pilgrim accounts

The earliest recorded account of a visit to the church is the Spanish pilgrim Egeria who visited in 383 AD and wrote:

"In Nazareth is a garden in which the Lord used to be after his return from Egypt, (Pet. Diac. Lib. P4) and there is a big and very splendid cave in which she (that is Holy Mary) lived. An altar has been placed there".[13]

Two years later, in 385 AD, the site was visited and reported on by the Christian scholar Jerome who described it as a 'mere village' (Latin *viculus*).

The basilica of Mary

In 431 AD there was an Ecumenical Church Council meeting in Ephesus in Turkey and on this occasion it was decreed that Mary was to be honoured as Jesus' mother. It is no surprise that later pilgrims report on a more developed site. The Piacenza Pilgrim in 570 AD stated: "The house of Saint Mary is now a basilica".[14] The outline of this Byzantine church can now be seen in the church. Pilgrim accounts were recorded after the Arab invasion of 638 AD.

The Crusader church

Following the Crusader invasion of 1099 AD, a large church was built on the site. This stood until 1263 AD when the Muslim Baybars demolished most of the site. The remains of the base walls can still be seen in the church today.

Mary's room?

For seven centuries pilgrims from all around the world have travelled to Loreto in Italy to a huge basilica that sits on top of a hill. Contained within its walls are the intact remains of a modest stone walled room said to be part of the original house of Mary. There is much controversy about this modest structure and the means by which it was allegedly transported from Palestine to Italy around 1291 AD. Some Catholic sources believe that the stones could be from the Nazareth area and their cutting could well be from the Early Roman Era. Saint Francis of Assisi (1181-1226 AD) made claims about this structure in Italy with its sacredness and its location.

The Franciscans - faithful custodians

St. Francis' order of monks became the inheritors of the sacred site in Nazareth and they have been faithful custodians of it since 1275 AD. Pilgrimages continued during the Medieval Era and in 1715 a substantial church was rebuilt on the site. This remained until the current structure was erected by the Franciscans in 1968.

---

13 Quoted by 'Peter the Deacon' in Taylor, JE 1993, *Christians and the Holy Places – The myth of Jewish-Christian origins*, Clarendon Press, Oxford, UK, p. 226

14 Murphy-O'Connor, J 1998, *The Holy Land*, Oxford University Press, Oxford, UK., p. 375.

Locating events in the life of Jesus

Reflection: Answered prayer

Mary's parents would have prayed for the location of their daughter's future residence. Mary was a devout Jewish woman and would also have prayed for the coming of the Messiah in her devotions in her residence.

Illus. 20 East view of the Catholic Church of the Annunciation located in Nazareth. Pilgrims visit this site from all around the world.

Illus. 21 View inside the Catholic Church of the Annunciation. The altar area marks the proposed location of the House of Mary.

5. JOSEPH'S HOME WORKSHOP – NV2

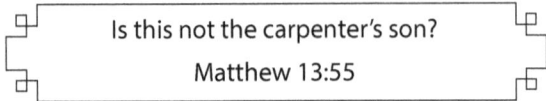

Is this not the carpenter's son?
Matthew 13:55

Location: St. Joseph's Workshop Church. In the main Catholic complex off Al-Bishara street at 32°42'11" N. and 35°17'54" E. A distance of 100 metres (110 yards) north of the Church of the Annunciation. The Franciscans have proposed this site as the family home and workshop but there is another explanation.

The synagogue leaders' exclamation above identifies Joseph as a carpenter. Teenage boys were apprenticed to their father or a relative to learn a trade or profession at about fifteen years of age. It is proposed that Joseph's *home workshop* was separate from his *public workshop* (No. 9, NC2) in Nazareth city (*refer* Appendix D.4). A carpenter requires a large shed for the drying and storing of timber. This facility would also be suitable for where Jesus and Joseph worked together to produce materials for their public workshop and shop-front (*refer* Appendix D.3). There was a need for a logistics base as there were no hardware stores as we know them today.

There is some uncertainty as to how broadly the Greek word '*tekton*' applied to Joseph and Jesus (Matt. 13:55, Mark 6:3). The common translation in the gospels is '*carpenter*' and even today that covers a wide range of activities.

The parcel of land

As well as the builder's yard there was a need for other amenities to provide for the family and conduct the business for twenty years. They would also need a stable for at least one and possibly more donkeys which would have been used for the transport of timber and tools to building sites. They might have kept other animals such as poultry, goats and sheep. The adjacent land could have been used to create gardens for the growing of some vegetables, vines and fruit trees. Joseph would have access to forest trees on the hill sides, and he may even have planted some of his own given his long tenure. All this requires a parcel of land of some size.

Jesus the student and helper

After returning from Egypt, Jesus as part of his growing up, would have attended a local school most probably in the urban sector. Jewish society in that era sent their children to a *bet ha-sefer* (school) to gain a good education. On school days Joseph and Jesus would have made the forty minute walk together. After school Jesus would have gone to Joseph's public workshop (NC2) and helped with jobs and the clean-up before returning home.

The later caretakers?

After Joseph's death Mary and Jesus depart from Nazareth in 28 AD. Their friends or relatives would be caretakers of the family home and gardens and may be responsible for the Early Roman remains and grotto found at this site. They would be part of the Judeo-Christian hamlet/village that developed in the locality after 30 AD which is explained in No. 8. There is some evidence of possible veneration in Byzantine times and remains of a Crusader church. Historical references of Joseph's connection date from the Medieval period.

Reflection: The prophetic cross beam

Christians over the centuries have commented on the boy Jesus growing up preparing wood and working with timber. As an apprentice he would have learnt to carry heavy beams and planks as part of his trade. He was a carpenter who hammered in lots of nails and was involved in constructing many frames and scaffolds. Jesus was a man who would become renowned as the one who carries his own cross beam, part of the way, as required of a Roman execution (John 19:17). He was a man who would eventually be nailed to a timber cross, the framing system so cruelly used by Roman law for crucifixion.

Illus. 22 Statue of St. Joseph outside the Workshop Church

Illus. 23 Entrance to St. Joseph's Workshop Church

6. JOSEPH'S FIRST BURIAL – NV3

> Is this not the carpenter, the Son of Mary, and brother to James, Joses, Judas, and Simon? And are not His sisters here with us?
>
> Mark 6:3

Location: Convent of the Sisters of Nazareth (NV3) off Al-Bishara street at 32°42'9" N and 35° 17'48" E. A distance of 70 metres (76 yards) west of the Church of the Annunciation. Map No. 2. p. 17. Limited access by appointment.

The above gospel reference shows that Jesus carried on the trade of his stepfather Joseph. The incident occurs during a visit to the city synagogue in September 27 AD (after Jesus had left his residence in the city). We are not told when Joseph died, but it would appear to be sometime before Jesus began his public ministry. Mary had probably shifted to a widow's community near Capernaum at the same time that Jesus relocated there. Jesus' new Galilee base near Capernaum would be a lodging provided by a friend or a relative (Matthew 4:13-16). The significance of the family home and Joseph's burial site was known to Mary and she would have ensured both sites were respected.

Illus. 24 Lead-light of the death of St. Joseph in the Workshop Church NV2.

A relative's tomb?

A question can be asked, where was the location of Joseph's first burial? There is a good possibility to consider with the discovery of burial places in the Convent of the Sisters of Nazareth in 1884.

- This site has a long history and a full survey was done by archaeologist Ken Dark in 2006.[15] The results showed that the site was originally the courtyard residence of a Jewish family in the Early Roman Era. It also revealed there were two first century tombs that were provided after the residence was abandoned. The subsequent evidence of Christian veneration has raised intriguing questions for this site.

---

15 Dark, K 2012, 'Early Roman–Period Nazareth and the Sisters of Nazareth Convent', *The Antiquaries Journal* 92, The Society of Antiquaries of London, UK. Ken Dark in this article proposes this site as the location of the house where Jesus grew up (Church of the Nutrition).

- An interesting feature of the burial site is the 'rolling stone' entrance to the tomb chamber which dates to the latter half of the first century (+50 AD).
- This tomb became part of a church in the Byzantine and Crusader eras. The obvious question is why did this occur? The answer may lie in the site's story given by locals to the 'Sisters' who built their convent there. The locals said, based on an unknown source, it was the location of the burial of a 'just man' or a 'saint'. Joseph is a good candidate to consider.
- The proposal is, if this site was an ancestral property (adjacent to the family home), it would be logical that it could be where Joseph's bones where initially stored. At a later period the 'rolling stone' tomb was provided to give a more secure but accessible location.
- There is an account that his remains were relocated to Bethlehem (*refer* Appendix D.5). If this is correct, the possible period would most likely have been towards the end of the Crusader era. This raises an interesting speculation, where in Bethlehem, his home city, could they be?

Reflection: Devout St. Joseph

There are traditions suggesting that Joseph was a humble man, not very rich and quite some years older than Mary. The few references to him point to a man who was devout and obedient to do the will of God. Some have suggested that Joseph died before Jesus began his ministry because his gentle soul would have found it hard to bear the intense opposition that Jesus faced with some of his ministry. The attempt to execute Jesus in Joseph's home city would be a good example of this point (explained in No. 11).

Illus. 25 Entrance to the Sisters of Nazareth Convent.

Illus. 26 Convent of the Sisters of Nazareth. Rolling stone tomb. Was it provided by Mary's relatives?

> The Rolling Stone tomb has all the features for a place of burial for St. Joseph. The evidence of subsequent veneration of the site supports this.

7. MARY'S NEIGHBOUR OR RELATIVE? – NV5

> Now Mary arose in those days and went into the hill country with haste, to a city of Judah and entered the house of Zacharias and greeted Elizabeth.
> Luke 1:39-40

Location: Mary of Nazareth International Center off Al-Bishara Street at 32°42' 8.8" N. and 35°17'47.4" E. A distance of 60 metres (65 yards) to the north of the Church of the Annunciation. *Refer* Map No. 2. p. 17.

The references to Mary's visit to Judea, and the later journey with Joseph and baby Jesus to Egypt imply some friends or relatives who look after their residence. Were there such people in their hamlet?

In 2011, this complex was opened with the support of twelve major Christian denominations in Israel. The aim was to have a centre that promoted an understanding of the Virgin Mary from different perspectives to cater to the diverse range of pilgrims from around the world. In the course of the site preparation, an amazing discovery was made of the remains of a historic residence. What excited the local Christians was the archaeologist's report that linked parts of it back to the Early Roman period. Yardenna Alexandre, the IAA archaeologist involved, has made some interesting observations:

> The discovery is of the utmost importance since it reveals for the first time a house from the Jewish village of Nazareth and thereby sheds light on the way of life at the time of Jesus. The building that we found was small and modest and is most likely typical of the dwellings in Nazareth in that period.[16]

This modest courtyard site with rooms, a cistern and a cave has been shown to be Jewish.

- It recently caused quite a stir as the Israeli Antiquities Authority dated the site from 100 BC to 100 AD which includes Mary's time frame from 19 BC to 42 (?) AD.
- These archaeological dates would make the site potential neighbours of Mary, Joseph and Jesus. The proximity could also provide a site for the later care-taking role for Mary and Joseph's home.
- It is most likely a residence of the Judeo-Christian community that formed after 30 AD which is explained next in No. 8.

---

16 Israel Antiquities Authority 2009, *For the Very First Time: A Residential Building from the Time of Jesus was Exposed in the Heart of Nazareth*, <www.antiquities.org.il/article_eng.aspx?sec_id=25&subj_id=240&id=1638>.

Reflection: A house of Prayer

If this residence was part of the Judeo-Christian community in the locality of the original home of Mary and Joseph it could have been occupied initially by one of their relatives. We know some of their names from Matthew 13: 54-56. Two of them, James (the Less) and Judas (known as Jude), became leaders in the early Christian Church. James was an apostle and the first bishop of the Judeo-Christian church and this role would mean he could have visited this site to pray with the occupants as part of his pastoral duties.

Illus. 27 Mary of Nazareth International Center on the left and Church of the Annunciation on the right. Courtesy www.cimdn.org. Left arrow indicates the ruins position. Right arrow indicates the dome above Mary's proposed house showing the proximity.

Illus. 28 Entrance sign

Illus. 29 Early Roman Era residence. Could this have been home to one of Mary's relatives?

8. THE FIRST CHURCH IN NAZARETH – NV4

> When He had come to His own country, He taught them in their synagogue, so that they were astonished and said, "Where did this Man get this wisdom and these mighty works? Is this not the carpenter's son? Is not His mother called Mary? And His brothers James, Joses, Simon and Judas? And His sisters, are they not all with us?   Matthew 13:54-56

Location: The 'Synagogue Church' in the Old Market off street No. 6120 at 32°42'11" N. and 35°17'48"E. It is 125 metres (140 yds) north of the Church of the Annunciation. Map No. 2. p. 17. The alleys may require asking a local.

Jesus' relatives

This gospel passage notes that Joseph was known as the 'father' of Jesus to some leaders in the synagogue and was also known to them. The main point in this passage is to note that there were at least four "brothers" and at least two "sisters" known to the leaders of the Nazareth Synagogue. There is much debate on the definition of these familial terms but the Greek word used is *'adelphoi'* which means from the *same womb*. However in Jewish society the term had a wider application and could include half-brothers, step-brothers and cousins. A careful examination of gospel references reveals they are cousins with Mary's mother (traditionally known as Anne) heading the family tree. Anne had two daughters named Mary (John 19:25)! The Virgin Mary's sister, also named Mary, was much older than her and was married to Clopas who produced children that were cousins (adelphoi) to Jesus. This was the understanding of early Church historians such as St. Jerome.

James (the Less) and Judas (Jude 1:1) both wrote New Testament books. These relatives and their descendants became known as the *'Desposyni'* which means in Greek, *belonging to the Master*. In 220 AD Julius Africanus, a historian, stated they were "so called because of their relation to the Saviour's family. *Living in the Jewish villages of Nazareth* and Cochaba" [italics added] (Eusebius *Church History* 9.1*)*. They are recorded in historical accounts as part of the Judeo-Christian community.

Illus. 30 James the Less, a cousin of Jesus. His father was Alphaeus not Joseph. (Luke 6:15) Wikimedia Commons.

Illus. 31 Entrances to the 'Synagogue Church' in the old market.
Access to the historical site is on the left.

The Judeo-Christian Community

For example at the end of the first century two grandsons of Jude (Judas) known as Zoker and Jacob are recorded as farming "thirty-nine plethra" (Eusebius *Church History* 3.20). Estimated as 8 hectares or 20 acres. This has been proposed as located in Nazareth by some scholars and the hamlet site would be the logical location. Their farm could include all the sites shown in Map No. 2. on page 17. Thus the grandsons of Jude may have inherited the estate of Mary and Joseph.

Visitors to Nazareth are shown a very historic church site in the Old Market or Suq area. The label on this site is the Nazareth Synagogue. However, as will be shown in No. 10 this cannot be the original synagogue in the time of Jesus (no Early Roman remains found). There is another explanation for this site:

- The existing structure is slightly below ground level and constructed of rusticated masonry in a barrel vault shape. The oldest part dates back to the Medieval period and this would pre-date 1771, when the Franciscans gave the site to the Melkite Christians. A test pit excavation inside the church in 1945 found remains that could date back to the Late Roman or early Byzantine periods.
- The locality was probably part of the early Judeo-Christian community and they may have designated some use for this site. In the fourth century this community went into decline and the inheritors of this site were the Gentile Christians known to us as the Byzantines. They could have established a site of devotion there.

A description of a site was found in the account of a pilgrim in 570 AD who stated:

> We travelled on to the city of Nazareth, where many miracles take place. In the synagogue there is kept the book in which the Lord wrote his ABC, and in this synagogue is the bench on which he sat with other children.[17]

The reference to Jesus' book and seat is ridiculous and more to do with the growing pilgrim trade. With the destruction of the Jewish Nazareth urban centre in 638 AD there was more logic to support all the Gospel sites to be at Christian Nazareth. This site would be reinforced as the location of Jesus' synagogue. Other accounts in 1137 AD and 1639 AD indicate that the current traditional site was the most likely place of veneration.

Illus. 32 Interior view of traditional Nazareth Synagogue. A spiritual site, but not the one associated with Jesus.

Reflection: The anointed place of worship

Some of the local Christians of Nazareth indicate that this site is very spiritual or anointed which they sense when visiting it. With the above explanation it can be seen why, as it has been a place of worship and prayer over many centuries. It has kept alive a tradition of a Nazareth synagogue even though it is not the correct location of the one associated with Jesus. For that reason it should be respected and honoured. The fact that pilgrims from many countries over many centuries have worshipped here explains the spiritual atmosphere.

---

17 Piacenza Pilgrim, Travels 5, Wilkinson, J (trans.) quoted in Murphy-O'Connor, J, 1998, *The Holy Land*, Oxford Archaeological Guides, Oxford University Press, Oxford, UK, p. 375.

Locating events in the life of Jesus

9. JOSEPH'S PUBLIC WORKSHOP? – NC2

> But while he thought about these things, behold an angel of the Lord appeared to him in a dream, saying, "Joseph, son of David, do not be afraid to take Mary your wife, for that which is conceived in her is of the Holy Spirit. And she will bring forth a Son, and you shall call His name Jesus for He will save His people from their sins".
>
> Matthew 1:20-21

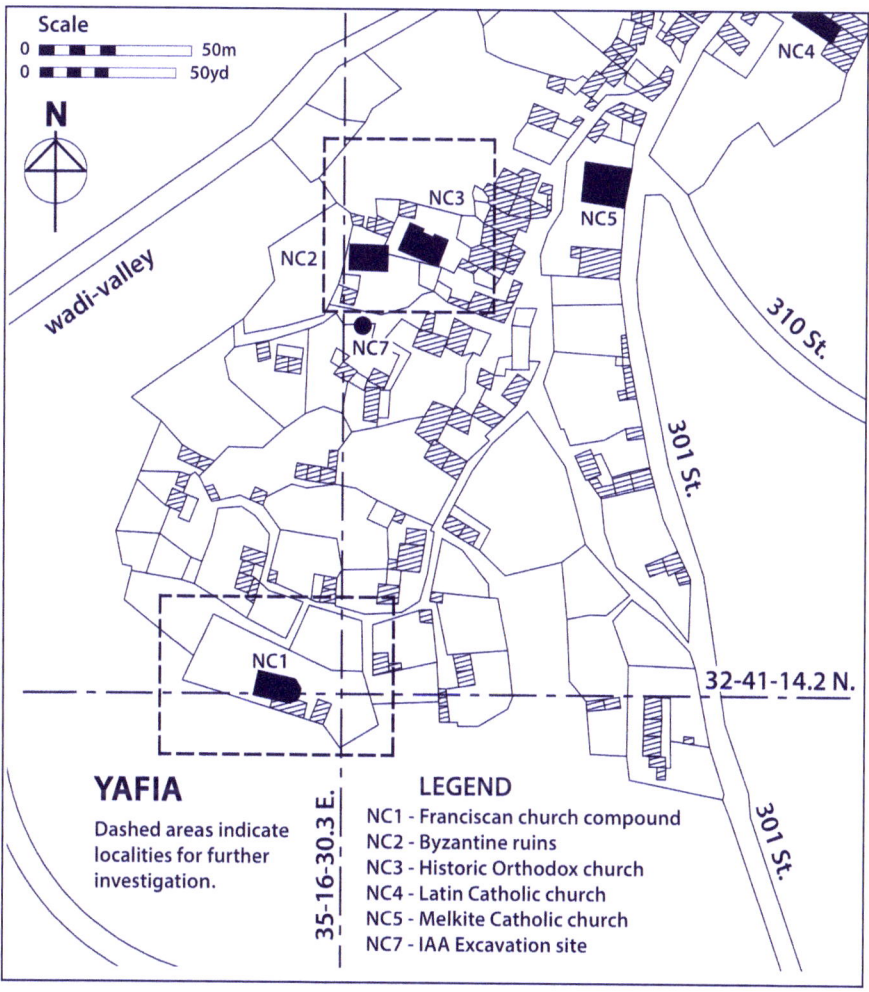

Illus. 33 Author map based on in the 1951 Yafia town survey in Sukenik, EL, 1951, *The Ancient Synagogue at Yafa near Nazareth*, The Hebrew university of Jerusalem, p. 11. Courtesy of the Institute of Archaeology, Hebrew University, Jerusalem.

Nazareth Gospel Sites

Illus. 34 Joseph's workshop recreated in Nazareth which is popular with tourists. Author's photo courtesy of the Nazareth Village. www.nazarethvillage.com.

Proposed locality: South of the new Orthodox church of Yafia located at 32°41'19" N. and 35°16'31" E. Just west of the historic St. George Orthodox church NC3. Buried (not accessible) under a modern housing block on piers.

Access: Via main road No. 75 to the traffic circle at Yafia. Off this circle is street No. 310, then street No. 305, then street No. 308. *Refer* Map No. 3. p. 9.

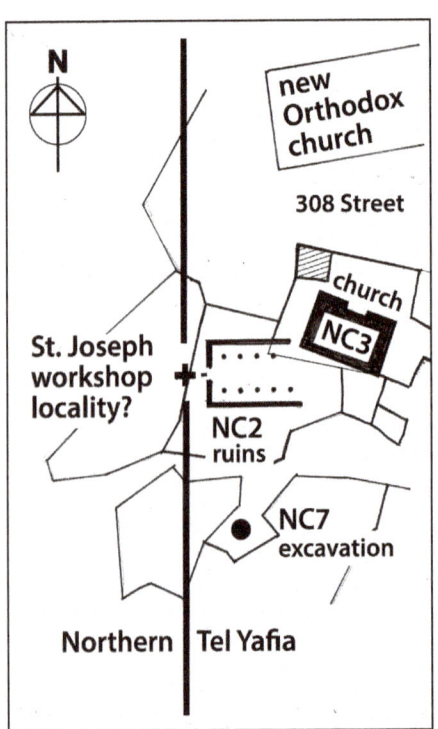

The account of an angelic visit to Joseph when he found out that Mary his betrothed wife was pregnant provides important information. First it confirms Joseph was a Nazarene being of the royal line of King David. Second the incident occurs in a location where Joseph is residing but separate from the location where Mary was living at the time. Where could this location be, given that Joseph was in *'erusin'*, a Jewish term for betrothal where he was legally married to Mary but not cohabiting at that stage? It was most likely that his bed was in his workshop in the urban centre.

Illus. 35 A sacred site (NC2) adjacent to Orthodox Church in Yafia (NC3). It is speculated that this locality may have contained St. Joseph's public workshop.

Count Joseph the Messianic Jew

The quest to find a locality where Joseph resided at the time of the angel's visit is an interesting challenge. Before this can be done there is an interesting person known in history who needs to be mentioned. There was a Jewish aristocrat from Tiberias who was converted to Christianity in about 333 AD and one of his passions was to build a Christian church in Nazareth. Scholars have debated whether he achieved his aim but with the correct identification of Jewish Nazareth a site has been found that shows he did achieve his aim. He had an interesting testimony which was recorded in an interview by a Cyprian bishop in 360 AD:

- He was born about 290 AD in a wealthy family and served a leading rabbi in Tiberias. After the death of this rabbi he found copies of the Christian Gospels in his library which surprised him. He read these and this began his journey of faith.

- Over the following years he made steps towards embracing the Christian faith but found a final commitment difficult. He finally had a dramatic conversion and became a Messianic Jew. Culturally he remained Jewish but his faith was strongly in Jesus as the Messiah.

Soon after he was granted an audience with Emperor Constantine who was impressed with his testimony. The Emperor gave him the title of a 'Count' and asked what favours he desired. Joseph's request was that:

> ... he be permitted by means of imperial edict to erect churches to Christ in the villages of the Jews. Indeed, no one had ever been able to build churches there, because neither Greek, nor Samaritan nor Christian was found in their midst ... This is true especially in Tiberias, in Diocesarea also known as Sefforis, *in Nazareth* and in Cafernaum ... but he fulfilled his building wishes in Diocesarea and some other cities [italics added]. [18]

Evidence for Count Joseph's church

The mystery of the location of his church was solved when a Byzantine structure was discovered in Yafia in 1951. The excavation by Professor Sukenik revealed a place of worship and he asked the question whether it was a pagan temple, a Jewish synagogue or a Christian church. His conclusion was a Jewish synagogue based on the floor mosaics showing they could be symbols of the twelve tribes of Israel. However he noted that the layout and orientation of the building was more like "a church" facing east rather than a synagogue. A proposal can be made that one of the mosaic floor panels discovered at the site is that of the Apostle John. His symbol in early Christian art was the eagle (*refer* Illus. 38). The mosaics of the twelve tribes would not be a

---

[18] 'Epiphanius', Donato Baldi, 1935, *Enchiridion Locorum Sanctorum, Jerusalem*, pp.2–3, Franciscan Cyberspot, <www.nazareth-en.custodia.org/default.asp?id=5952>

problem for a Messianic Jew and they are also listed in the Apostle John's Book of the Revelation (Rev. 7:5-8). A more detailed account explaining this building as that of Count Joseph in Byzantine Nazareth has been given.[19]

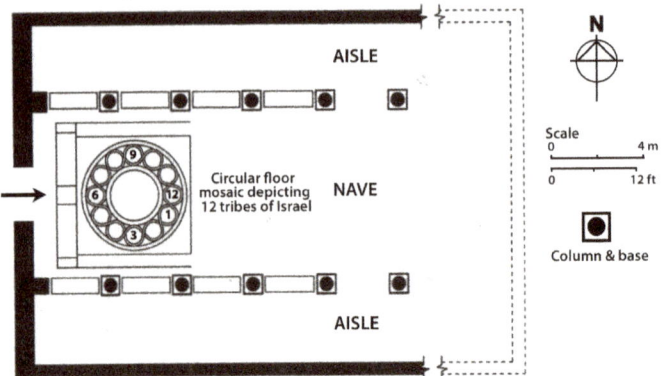

Illus. 36 Yafia 'Synagogue' plan drawn by author based on E.L. Sukenik archaeology report. Note the 12 circular mosaics that Sukenik identified as Jewish tribal symbols.

Illus. 37 Author with column base and capital from Yafia Byzantine sacred archaeological site.

Illus. 38 Yafia mosaic depicting a young man's face (with scroll and eagle) proposed as John the Evangelist. This gives support for this being a Christian site

Saint Joseph's city workshop and shop-front

The points supporting the proposal, albeit speculative are given:
- Devout Count Joseph would have prayed for guidance for the location of his church. There may have been a local Christian tradition, passed down that preserved the spiritual significance of the site. Just reflect on some of the sermons that could have been preached at this site in the heart of the city that Jesus grew up in.

---

19 Harris, T op. cit. pp. 106–118. An estimate of Count Joseph's time frame of building is 340-350 AD. The image of John above is very similar to one of him in the Celtic Lindisfarne Gospels.

- Located adjacent and west of the Orthodox church in Yafia shows a long continuity of worship in the locality. They may have inherited the site after the great Schism of 1054 AD.
- The site is on the northern slopes of the city outside the city walls. Joseph's future home was located to the north-east. This is a logical place for a trades-person to do business being near the city gates. It is 50 metres (54 yards) from the proposed city walls.
- An archaeological excavation was done recently thirty metres to the south of the site. The results showed: "Silos and underground cavities associated with a settlement from the Early Roman period were exposed in the excavation".[20]
- Even if remains of a workshop were found it would still be speculative that it belonged to Joseph. (*Refer* Appendix D.4 for an interesting comment.) This locality is a good candidate for further investigation.

Illus. 39 Early Roman remains found under the Catholic Church in Yafia NC4. This site is located in the suburban area of Nazareth city in 27 AD. Other similar evidence has been found in excavations around Tel Yafia.

Reflection: A site of Blessing

As every trades-person will tell you, it is not just the skill that counts when making a living, but it is also about getting and retaining clients. Jesus would have watched how Joseph acquired his customers and how he handled their different temperaments and expectations. He would have learnt the importance of patience and persistence. This was part of growing up in wisdom and stature (Luke 2:52). In his work and in his relationships, he was a source of blessing and favour to others. Having served his apprenticeship, Jesus would gradually have been given more responsibility in the business. This would have required him to travel in the region around Nazareth, finding new clients and visiting building sites. Historical tradition suggests that Joseph was quite old by the time Jesus was twenty, so this would result in more responsibility being given to him as the only son.

---

20 Zidan, O 2015, Yafi'a, *Hadashot Arkheologiyot, Israel Antiquities Authority*, Volume 127, p. 3.

10. THE NAZARETH SYNAGOGUE – NC1

> When He had come to his own country, He taught them in their synagogue, so that they were astonished and said "Where did this Man get this wisdom and these mighty works? Is this not the carpenter's son? … Where then did this Man get all these things?" So they were offended at Him. But Jesus said to them, "A prophet is not without honor except in his own country and in his house". Now He did not do many mighty works there because of their unbelief.
>
> Matthew 13:54-58

Introduction

This account indicates that Jesus found some of his hometown citizens not very receptive to his teaching. Hence the proverb, still used today, that prophets are often not recognised by their own people. The response of the congregation shows that Jesus was known to them, but not in an exceptional way as he was part of the large congregation, not that of a small hamlet or village. He had worshipped there for twenty two years but would be looked down on as being of a working-class trade.

Factors for a location

When the correct locality of urban Nazareth is established the site of its main synagogue needs to be explored. The following factors give support for a particular locality to be investigated. A good location is in the south-western end of Tel Yafia (*refer* Appendix D.6):

- The gospel indicates that Jesus was seized at the synagogue and then thrust out of the city. This would locate a position somewhere inside the main elevated plateau with the city walls around the perimeter.
- Excavations for existing building foundations have not revealed any remains of a Early Roman Era synagogue. The northern section of the plateau has dense housing which eliminates 80% of the required area. The only open areas are in the southern sector.
- It would be logical that the early pioneers of Nazareth would have located their synagogue in a central and prominent location. It would be a focal point in their community.
- In the study of historical urban and regional planning there is the principle of '*land-use succession*'. This shows that successive historical periods often re-use sites of previous generations. For example roads tend to follow previous tracks and houses tend to be built on former dwellings. When it comes to sacred sites it is quite common to find previous sacred sites being re-used, regardless of the religion.

Locating events in the life of Jesus

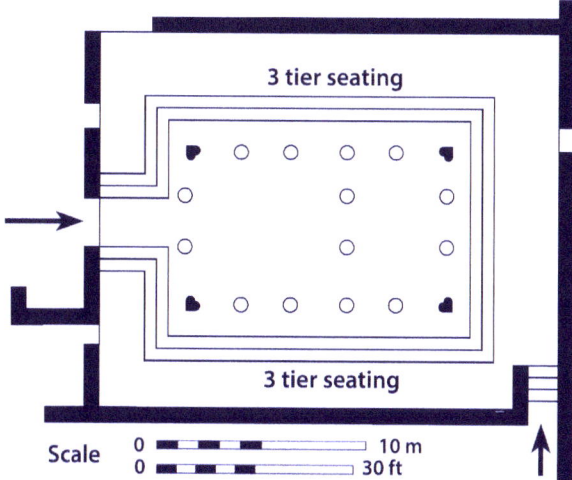

Illus. 40 Gamla Synagogue in the Golan region north-east of the Sea of Galilee.
This structure existed until demolition by the Romans in 67 AD.
The hall size was 22 x 17m or 72 x 55 feet. Author's plan based on Spigel, CS, 2012 *Ancient Synagogue Seating Capacities,* Mohr Siebeck, Tubingen, Germany, p. 80. Spigel calculated that the seating capacity could be for 344 people based on certain assumptions.

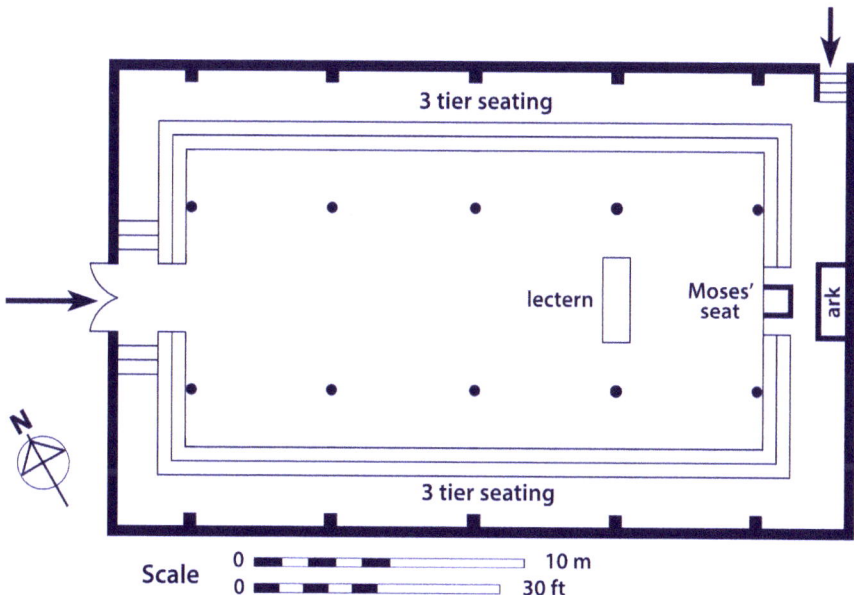

Illus. 41 Author's plan of proposed Nazareth Synagogue, 27 x 17 metres – 88 x 55 feet.
Three tiered seating for 400 people could be provided. Extra overflow bench seats could be put at the side walls. A timber frame structure for the internal posts is shown to reduce the visual impact. Jesus would have read from the Isaiah scroll at the lectern.

The historic Franciscan site - NC1

Location: Southern peak of Tel Yafia at 32°41'14.2" N. and 35°16'29.6" E.

Access: Via main road No. 75 to the traffic circle at Yafia. Off this circle is street No. 310 then street No. 305 leads towards the site. Arrow signs indicate "Mar Yarkob". It can be difficult to find so ask a local. *Refer* Map No. 3 p. 9.

Illus. 42 Franciscan Church in Yafia commemorating the apostles James and John. The orientation of the building and compound is towards Mt. Precipice / Kedumim.

The previous factors give support for the locality of the Franciscan Church compound. It is a good candidate to start investigation for a synagogue. It is located on the high point in the south-west corner of the elevated plateau. It is known as the Church of the Holy Apostles due to a tradition that it was the original residence of the sons of Zebedee, the apostles James and John. This tradition can be shown as incorrect. The archaeologist B. Bagatti has documented part of its history. A Franciscan chapel existed there in 1766 and was replaced with the existing church in 1885. The church and the compound do not face east as many churches do but towards the peak of Mount Kedumim (Mt. Precipice). There are plans afoot to develop this site which would require a full survey. This site and its surrounding area is definitely worthy of further investigation.

Illus. 43 The peak of Tel Yafia facing west. NC1 indicates the historic Franciscan Church.

Locating events in the life of Jesus

Illus. 44 'Jesus unrolls the book in the Synagogue' painting by James Tissot circa1886. Credit: Brooklyn Museum photograph 2007.

Reflection: The Messiah prays

Jesus grew up worshipping with his parents in the city synagogue. As part of the worship service the congregation would have a time of prayer where they would stand and face Jerusalem. This standing prayer was called the *Amidah* which involved a series of set prayers. The origin of these prayers went back to the time of Ezra in the fifth century BC. One of these prayers was known as the 'Blessing of David'. The format of the prayer was to pray for the coming of the Messiah. A modern translation of this prayer is: "Cause the progeny [descendant] of David your servant, to blossom quickly. Let him shine in your deliverance, for we await your salvation every day".[21] Thus Jesus as part of the congregation would have stood with his fellow worshippers and faced Jerusalem and spoke a similar prayer for the salvation plan of the Messiah.

---

21 Hoffman, LA 1997, *My People's Prayer Book: The Amidah,* Jewish Lights Publishing, Woodstock, Vermont, USA, p. 142, </books.google.com.au/books?id=9_akQQPpS9IC>.

11. THE NAZARETH EXECUTION LOCALITY – NC8

Illus. 45 'The plan to kill Jesus" Jerome Nadal 1595 AD.
<http://catholic-resources.org/Nadal/040.jpg>.

Luke 4: 16-30

Then Jesus returned in the power of the Spirit to Galilee, and the news of Him went out through all the surrounding region. And He taught in their synagogues, being glorified by all. So he came to Nazareth, where He had been brought up. And as His custom was, He went into the synagogue on the Sabbath day, and stood up to read. And He was handed the book of the prophet Isaiah. And when He opened the book, He found the place where it was written:

"The Spirit of the LORD is upon Me,
Because He has anointed Me
To preach the gospel to the poor;
He has sent Me to heal the brokenhearted,
To proclaim liberty to the captives
And recovery of sight to the blind.
To set at liberty those who are oppressed;
To proclaim the acceptable year of the LORD".

Then He closed the book, and gave it back to the attendant and sat down. And the eyes of all who were in the synagogue were fixed on Him. And He began to say to them, "Today this Scripture is fulfilled in your hearing". So all bore witness to Him, and marveled at the gracious words which proceeded out of His mouth. And they said, "Is this not Joseph's son?"…

(Some time later after further teaching there was a different reaction).

… So all those in the synagogue, when they heard these things, were filled with wrath, and rose up and thrust Him out of the city; and they led Him to the brow of the hill on which the city was built, that they might throw Him down over the cliff. Then passing through the midst of them, He went His way.

Prophets not accepted in their hometown
Jesus' second return visit to the Nazareth synagogue was far more dramatic. On this occasion it was the solemn Day of Atonement and this coincided with the Gospel declaration at the evening start of the Jubilee. Jesus' implied claim to be the Messiah caused great surprise. He had quoted Isaiah's prophecy (61:1-2) and stated he was the fulfilment of it. Later some of his fellow citizens took strong exception to his teaching and there was an attempt to execute him. The evidence for the location of these events can be presented.

Proposed locality: Notional coordinates: 32°40'52" N. and 35°15'56" E. The southern slopes of Yafia Valley just over one kilometre (1100 yards) south-west from Tel Yafia. (Adjacent to a residential area so discretion is required).
Access: Via main road No. 75 to the last western traffic circle and petrol station in Yafia. Turn into street No. 111, then first left into a cul-de-sac to the end, then in bushland located 150 metres to the west. Partially viewable 275 metres (300 yds) north-west of the petrol station. *Refer* Map No. 1 p. 9.

The points in favour of this locality are:
- Mt. Precipice is a favourite site with its steep slopes and spectacular view of the Jezreel Valley but it does not meet the Gospel requirements. Why would such a great picnic and lookout site be used for executions?
- The common ridge with the city, as seen in Illus. 47 runs to the south-west of Tel Yafia. The Greek word in the gospel text is translated as "brow" and is the same word used for eyebrow, denoting the profile of the prominence. The brow is the cusp of a ridge with a steep slope falling away as shown in Illus. 48.
- The watercourse on the western side of Tel Yafia flows south-west so this is the logical direction for any sewage from the city. The main water supply to the city was north-west so these two factors support a ritually unclean execution site to be south-west.
- Under Jewish law a measure for being ritually separated was 2,000 cubits which is about 890 metres (972 yards). This was the measure used to keep the Israelites separate from the holy Ark when they crossed the Jordan (Joshua 3:4). (It was also the measure for a Sabbath day's journey.)

The Jewish Stoning place
Most Jewish cities had a dedicated stoning place to execute people judged to be in breach of particular laws. *Refer* Appendix D.7. These sites are mentioned in Jewish history books and one account stated: "The stoning area's height was that of two men. One of the witnesses pushed him on his loins" (Mishnah Sanhedrin 6:4). The Gospel account uses a Greek word that indicates that the intended execution of Jesus was to "cast down headlong" which explains this action. The proposed execution site can now be described:

- A deep crevice in the ridge is required of sufficient depth to allow a fall of 4 metres (14 feet) from the tipping rail (two men height plus balustrade).
- A scaffolding bridge is required to allow for the headlong fall and provide safety to the executioners.
- The headlong fall quickly rendered the offender unconscious or dead. They were then checked, and if not dead, the witnesses participated in a group stoning to ensure death as prescribed in Deuteronomy 17:7.
- This was seen as a quick and humane way for serious law-breakers to be executed with community justice.
- This crevice would be difficult to locate today as seismic activity and natural erosion have caused infilling and altered the landscape. The site would have been abandoned in the seventh century when the Jewish city was decimated. The nominal position is north of an existing dump site.

A reconstructed scenario

With the preceding factors, a convincing narrative of the dramatic events can be made. The Day of Atonement was at the end of September in 27 AD (sunset to sunset on the next day). That evening at sunset the trumpet (shofar) was sounded to commence the very sacred day and assembly. This was the service where Jesus made his Jubilee declaration, much to their amazement. The following day was still the holy day and services continued in the synagogue. Jesus also gave teaching that afternoon, and on this occasion some attendees took strong exception to his message. This caused heated debate and anger. However being a holy day they could not execute him as no such work could be done on a Sabbath.

As the sun set that evening, the holy day ended with a trumpet blast and some members would have made their way home. Refreshments may have been taken by those remaining. However there was a group that was not happy, in particular the leaders, probably Pharisees and their friends. They were "filled with wrath" and formed a circle around Jesus. An animated discussion occurred and they confronted him. How dare he, the local carpenter's son challenge them on matters of faith. The rulers took counsel and deemed him worthy of execution. There was no legal trial as was required under Jewish law but what we in Australia call a *'kangaroo court'*, an unjust hasty trial, such was the intensity of the wrath.

If the seating of the synagogue was four hundred then a crowd of about two hundred could be involved, with leaders whipping up emotions. With fading light (and darkness falling), burning torches would have been produced to give light. Eventually Jesus was seized, but not bound, and physically escorted from the synagogue precinct. He went voluntarily, and was "thrust out of the city" (v.28). Emotions were running high as the mob with flickering torches made their way outside the city into the darkness.

Locating events in the life of Jesus

Illus. 46 The angry mob heading to the scaffold platform and deep crevice in the ridge. The offender was dropped headlong.

Illus. 47 Nazareth city from the south showing the ridge connecting the city and the proposed execution site (NC8) as required in the gospel account.
Base map Google Earth. Image © 2015 DigitalGlobe.

They moved south-westerly along a narrow path towards the execution site on the eastern side of the valley. This valley echoed the howling and yelling of the mob. The execution site was some distance away involving a fifteen minute walk. The rocky parts and crevices required careful navigation to prevent a trip or fall. They headed towards the main sewage dump with its pungent odour filling the air.

They were moving towards the deep crevice with a platform with railing that formed a sheer drop. The crowd was pushing and shoving and highly agitated. At a point in the walk before they reached this site Jesus simply stopped. In the poor light, those pushing behind took their eyes off him to navigate a rocky section. They pressed past him not noticing his action. As they marched past Jesus stood till the last member passed in the poor light. [22] He then slipped away and returned to his home in Capernaum. This is how "passing through the midst of them, He went His way" (v.30). It was not a bizarre leap as one tradition suggests.

Reflection: A premature execution

The plot to kill Jesus before his appointed time had other examples in the Gospels. The leaders in Jerusalem considered the same (Mark 3:6). The Jewish leaders were wanting the coming of the Messiah but a political one with their expectations.

Illus. 48 View from Franciscan compound (NC1) towards proposed execution site (NC8).

---

22 The author acknowledges the account referenced in footnote No. 32. Schmoger, C. vol. 2, p. 236.

12. THE TRANSFIGURATION ON MT. TABOR – T1

> Now after six days Jesus took Peter, James and John his brother, led them up the mountain by themselves, and He was transfigured before them. His face shone like the sun, and His clothes became as white as the light. And behold, Moses and Elijah appeared to them, talking with Him.   Matthew 17: 1-3

Which holy mountain?

There is a strong case for Mount Tabor being the location of this event. The apostle Peter recalling the event said: "And we heard this voice which came from heaven when we were with Him on the holy mountain" (2 Peter 1:18).

The early Church scholar Origen (185-254 AD) said: "Thabor is the mountain of Galilee on which Christ was transfigured"(Comm. In Ps lxxxviii, 13). This was followed by "St. Cyril of Jerusalem (Catechetical lectures II.16) and St. Jerome (Epistles 46, 53 and 23) likewise declare it categorically." [23]

The spiritual significance of this mountain is well known. The north-west quarter of its slopes was designated to the Levite priests of Daberath. Deborah and Barak used it as their headquarters in their campaign against the Canaanites (Judges 4:6). It had a long history as a place of worship and devotion (Hosea 5:1).

There are currently a number of venerated sites on Mount Tabor but there are two in particular that are worthy of attention. [24]

Mount Tabor access: From Nazareth and Iksal to Daburiya. Road No. 7266 up the western side of Mount Tabor. A better longer road is No. 60 to Afula then No. 65, and then left hand turn-off to road No. 7266 takes you to the summit.

Illus. 49 View to Mt. Tabor from Mt. Kedumim. IS17 marks Horbat Devora located near modern Daburiya and Z5 marks Chisloth-Tabor on the southern slopes.

---

23 Newadvent.org. 2016, *Catholic Encyclopedia*, 'Transfiguration'.
24 Illus. 50. The Cave of Melchizedek (T5) which dates to the Crusader period. It is based on a tradition at that time that this enigmatic figure may have had occasion to visit the mount in his travels. The other site is the Medieval Decentibus chapel (T6) which preserves the tradition of the descent of the disciples after the transfiguration.

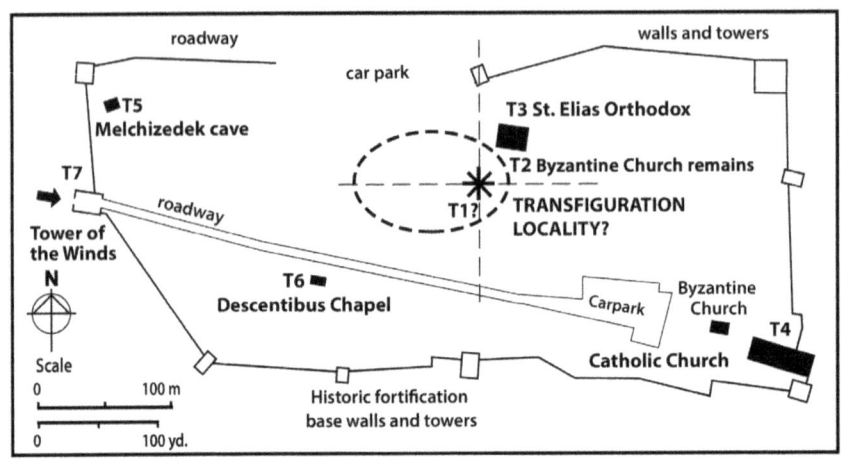

Illus. 50 Mt. Tabor sacred sites and proposed transfiguration locality for investigation. Fortifications credit after Battista & Bagatti in Pringle, D 1998 *The Churches of the Crusader Kingdom of Jerusalem*, vol. II, Cambridge University Press, UK.

The Orthodox compound of Saint Elias – T3.

Location: St. Elias Church at 32°41'16.2" N. and 35°23'25" E.

Access: Near the summit before reaching the Tower of the Winds gateway turn left to the northern side. There is only authorised access to this monastery and church.

This site includes the remains of a Byzantine church in the southern compound that dates back to the fourth century. It was recorded by the pilgrim of Piacenza in 570 AD and in 1102 AD the pilgrim Saewulf observed:

"On the summit still remain three ancient monasteries; one in honour of our Lord Jesus Christ; another in honour of Moses, and a third at some distance from the others, in honour of Elias." [25]

The Orthodox southern compound and areas westward has remains of ancient grottos, some of which may still be sealed after the Muslim victory over the Crusaders in 1183 AD. This locality is favoured by the author for further investigation as there appears to be a prophetic signpost to the north. This is Joshua's city site called Japhia, known today as Horbat Binit located at 32°44'49" N. and 35°23'25" E. The meaning of Japhia is "God shines," a description that will resonate with Christians as the site pointing to Jesus' transfiguration. *Refer* also to Appendix E.

---

[25] Bohn, HG 1848. *Early travels in Palestine*, George Woodfall and Son. London, p. 46. This account would suggest that the site of Saint Elias is a historic one and could date back to the Byzantine era. This would then link it to one of the three basilicas noted in 570 AD.

Locating events in the life of Jesus

Illus. 51 View towards the Orthodox Church compound southern wall. This locality is supported as the proposed location of the grotto of the transfiguration. Remains of a Byzantine Church have been found adjacent.

The Catholic Church of the Transfiguration – T4.

Location: On the eastern side of the Tabor plateau at 32°41'10.5" N. and 35°23'30" E.

Access: Via the road No. 7266 through the Tower of the Winds gateway, along the main avenue to the car-park at the end. Public access at set times. *Refer* map Illus. 50.

This massive church structure, by the famed Italian architect Antonio Barluzzi was built in 1924 and dominates the summit as a landmark to the region. Adjacent are church remains dating back to Byzantine times that are recorded in history and mentioned by pilgrims over the ages. This site being very accessible to pilgrims has played a major role in preserving the story of the gospel accounts. Mount Tabor was sacred to the Jews and some of the grottos of this locality would have been used by the prophets and pilgrims before the time of Jesus. Such candidates would be the prophets Malachi, a resident of Zebulun, Nahum a resident of Naphtali and Elijah who was a resident of Mount Carmel. It is no surprise that Elijah was one of those who met Jesus on the mount.

Levite Daberath

Location: Horvat Devora north of the city of Daburiyeh on the north-west side of the Tabor plateau at 32°41'50.2" N. and 35°22'39" E.

This site was allocated to Levite priests of Issachar. They were required to provide accurate dedicated boundary markers to their city and suburbs. It is proposed that one of these northern markers was a prophetic signpost pointing to the incarnation. This is illustrated in Illus. 59 on page 60.

Illus. 52 Mt. Tabor Byzantine church remains adjacent to the modern Catholic Church.

Reflection: The story of the glory

The three selected disciples Peter, James, and John travel with Jesus to Xaloth, (Chisloth Tabor), a site noted by Josephus, at the southern base of Mount Tabor. They ascend the southern side of the mount and arrive at the elevated peak plateau which today has a Catholic Church. The position is commanding and there are ancient grottos and caves. These are the places of retreat and prayer used by prophets mentioned previously.

As evening begins to fall Jesus and his disciples move north-west to the centre of the plateau near the current southern compound of the Orthodox Church. Somewhere near this compound and its adjacent gardens is the grotto where the transfiguration occurred. The meeting of the spirit bodies of Moses representing the law and Elijah representing the prophets occurs. In the morning they descend the north-western pathway to the Roman Era Levite city of Daberath. The disciples were told not to recall the event until after the resurrection of Jesus. The apostle John later wrote: "And the Word became flesh and dwelt among us, and we beheld His glory as the begotten of the Father, full of grace and truth" (John 1:14). [26]

---

[26] The author acknowledges that parts of this account are based on information in footnote reference No. 32. vol. 3, pp. 295-301.

APPENDICES

APPENDIX A: OTHER SITES OF INTEREST

Mary's Well–NV7

Location: Mary's Well Square off Paulus VI street north end at 32°42'22" N. and 35°18'5" E.

A traditional site located 600 metres (656 yards) to the north-west of the Catholic Church of the Annunciation. This would suggest this was not the main source of Mary's water. There is debate on the age of this site but there is evidence that it was used in Late Roman and Byzantine times. It would have been a popular place for pilgrims to camp over the centuries. The well has been an iconic image for traditional Nazareth village and featured on many historic postcards.

Historic Bathhouse–NV8

Location: Adjacent to Mary's Well Square at 32°42'22.5" N. and 35°18'5" E.

Remains of a historic bathhouse were found near Mary's well in the 1990's. There is debate about the exact date of this structure but there is evidence that this could date to the Roman Era. Features of this era in the facility include a warming bath (hypocaust) has raised speculation as to who the builders could be. It may have been part of an inn used by Gentile Christians who were pilgrims to the site in the Late Roman era. It would be on the outskirts of the Judeo-Christian community centred on the traditional Catholic site.

Orthodox Church of Saint Gabriel–NV6

Location: Adjacent to Mary's Well Square at 32°42'25" N. and 35°18'5.5" E.

In the Orthodox tradition this was the location of the annunciation of Mary at a spring found under the structure. Remains date back to the Byzantine era for this site and later it was rebuilt in the Crusader era.

Nazareth Village Project–NV9

Location: Off Paulus VI street, off Al Wadi Al Jawani Street, to street No. 5079 south of the hospital at 32°42'0" N. and 35°17'31.6 E. *Refer* Map No. 1 p. 9.

An interesting complex in recent years has been developed about six hundred metres (656 yards) to the west of the hamlet site. It is called the Nazareth Village and located on a historic farm that dates back to the first century BC. A team of archaeologists led by Stephen Pfann and Ross Voss have explored and developed the site which was opened in the year 2000. At the centre of the project is the re-creation of a typical Galilean village with houses, workshops and a synagogue. Locals are employed and dressed to depict aspects of the Jewish lifestyle of the first century. It is a very popular site with visiting tourists seeking a glimpse of what life would have been like in Jesus' time.

APPENDIX B: THE HISTORY OF TWO NAZARETHS

Date/ Historical Era*	Nazareth Walled City NC	Nazareth Village NV
Pre-Canaanite	Prehistoric cave sites at Mt. Precipice / Kedumim nearby both sites	
Early Bronze	No occupation	No occupation
End Middle Bronze (MBIIC) 1450–1400 BC	Small Israelite hamlet. MBII remains found.	Small Israelite hamlet. MBII remains found.
Late Bronze 1400–1120 BC	Small hamlet occupation	Small hamlet occupation
Iron Age 1120–732 BC	Small hamlet occupation	Small hamlet occupation
Eastern Empires 732–332	Abandoned	Abandoned
Hellenistic 332–63 BC Maccabees about 100 BC	Devout Nazarene Jewish village named Nazareth in 100–80 BC	Small devout Jewish farm area linked to main Nazarene village 2.5km (1.5 mi.) to S.W.
Early Roman 63 BC–135 AD Includes Jesus' Era 4 BC–30 AD	Large Jewish walled city named Nazareth starts about 80 BC. City of Joseph and Mary.	Devout Jewish hamlet of Mary & Joseph 4 BC–27 AD. Becomes Christian after 30 AD.
Late Roman 135–325 AD	Decline after 70 AD. Minimal Jewish site affected by two wars. Revived Jewish city after 313 AD.	Small Judeo-Christian hamlet. Jewish & Roman opposition.
Byzantine 325–638 AD	345 AD Count Joseph's church. 377 AD Devout Jewish town. Record of Nazareth priests. 630 AD Dispersal of Jews written by Jewish poet Eleazar ben Killir	Small Christian 'Village of the Saviour' mentioned by Jerome c. 400 AD. Growth of the city and basilica of Mary's house 570 AD. Growth of pilgrims.
Islamic Arab Period (Umayyad, Abbasid) 640–1099 AD	Largely abandoned site with few remains. Memory of the city begins to fade, then lost.	Small Christian village visited by pilgrims. Mentioned in travellers' diaries.
Crusader 1099–1291 AD	Small village. Unknown name. Nearby village 3.2 km (2 mi.) to the north called Japheth in Greek and Ophna in Hebrew.	Large Christian city. Catholic basilica at centre with pilgrims giving descriptions. Destroyed 1263 AD, remains found.
Islamic–Medieval (Ayyubid, Mamluk) 1291–1517 AD	Village named Safra and Saron. Proposed tradition of birthplace Apostles James & John. 1350 AD.	Small Christian village noted by pilgrims.
Islamic–Ottoman 1517–1917 AD	Village known as Saffa/Safra. Orthodox & Catholic Churches. Robinson endorses as Yafa 1841.	Christian village with some pilgrims. Preliminary surveys by Quaresmius 1626 AD.
British Mandate 1917–1948 AD	Christian–Muslim village known as Yafia. 1948 receives many Arab refugees from nearby Mual area.	Christian town of Nazareth. Many pilgrims. Catholic, Orthodox and Protestant churches.
Modern Israel 1948 AD – Present	Muslim–Christian suburb of greater Nazareth city. IAA archaeological survey confirms large Early Roman city remains.	Large Israeli city. Major rebuild of Church of the Annunciation in 1968 AD. Large numbers of worldwide pilgrims.

* Dates based on Murphy-O'Connor, J op. cit. pp. 2-5. (Exception lower Iron Age date of 1120 BC based on other scholars proposals.) Some also date the Early Roman Era from 37 BC.

APPENDIX C: HOW NAZARETH BECAME YAFIA/JAPHIA

Two important facts need to be established. The first is how the urban Nazareth site became known as Yafia (Japhia). The second is the correct location of biblical Japhia.

Early tensions

After 30 AD the divide between Jews and Christians began to grow with many Jews not accepting Jesus as the Messiah. The hamlet site would have been a community of devout Judeo-Christians. The urban site would have remained Jewish.

Jewish priests at Nazareth

In 1962 a fragment of a wall plaque was found at Caesarea which contained the name of Nazareth. It was shown to be part of a fragment that read: *"The 18th course Hapizzez Nazareth"*. Scholars have accepted that this was evidence of a group of Jewish priests, in the fourth century who lived in Nazareth, which would have been the urban site. The Israeli Government Mint issued a medallion in 1981 commemorating this fragment. This is historic evidence of the name of Nazareth outside of Christian sources.

Illus. 53 Hebrew text by M. Avi-Yonah showing fragment found in Caesarea listing Nazareth. Author's copy of Israel Nature and Parks Authority text.

Illus. 54 Israeli Government Mint Medallion showing the Nazareth fragment. The Hapizzez text above is written around the edge.

Growth of Gentile Christianity

The rise of Gentile Christianity and the conversion of Constantine in 313 AD had a dramatic effect. His capital Constantinople ruled the Byzantine Empire and included former Roman Palestine. This empires rule became oppressive to the Jews in the seventh century.

The destruction of Nazareth

In 614 AD the Persian king Chosroes II attacked Palestine and killed many Christians. He was aided by some of the local Jews who attacked the Christian community at Nazareth. In 630 AD the Byzantines returned: "In revenge, the emperor Heraclius reluctantly singled out Nazareth for special punishment".[27] Thus the Jewish city was decimated and became lost in time.

The lament over Nazareth

This event was recorded by a Jewish poet, Eleazar ben Killir whose *Lamentations* were read in synagogues for many centuries. His time frame has been dated by some sources from 570–640 AD. He wrote:
"And to the ends of the earth was dispersed the priestly class of Nazareth".[28]

Illus 55 A Street sign in modern Tel Aviv named after poet El'Azar (Ha) Kalir.
Credit Wikimedia Commons.

The Crusader era

During this period a site known as Shefar'am (Safra) developed on the pilgrim route from Akko to Nazareth. It was suggested that this site was the location of the home of the apostles James and John, the sons of Zebedee.

The Medieval–Ottoman period

After the defeat of the Crusaders by the Muslims the name of Safra and its legend was transferred to the hill of Yafia. This was noted by the archaeologist B. Bagatti who wrote: "This privilege then passed onto Yafia near Nazareth where it remains until our day." [29]

Jafa and Yafa

In the Crusader era there was a site known as Japheph near Nazareth (proposed as Z47, Illus. 04). This along with Yafa led to the hill near Nazareth being known as Yafa or Jafa. When the American explorer Edward Robinson visited the site in 1841 he confirmed this as his nomination of biblical Japhia. This sealed the fate of Nazareth and Bible atlases continue this error today.

---

27 Taylor, J 1993, *Christians and the Holy Places – The myth of Jewish–Christian origins*, Clarendon Press, Oxford, UK., p. 229.
28 Tuccinardi, E 2010, *Nazareth the Caesarea Inscription and the hand of God*, Salm, R (trans.), p. 10.
29 Bagatti, B 2001, *Ancient Christian Villages of Galilee*, Jerusalem: Franciscan Printing Press. Jerusalem, p. 106

Yafia as Japhia not accepted by scholars

There are a number of leading scholars who have not accepted the nomination of Yafia as biblical Japhia. This is based on the order in Joshua 19:10-14 and the topographic logic. The reasons were summarised by Professor Yigal Levin who concluded: *"For these reasons many scholars remain undecided on the identification of Japhia."* [italics added] [30]

Jafia is located at Ilaniya

There is evidence that reveals a more logical location for Japhia being the locality of modern Ilaniya (Z8, Illus.03). It meets the biblical requirement of being north of Mount Tabor and has support from the archaeology. The relationship between biblical Japhia and the fortress site of Jotapata at Khirbet Atosh according to Josephus' descriptions can be determined. Tel Yodfat is not the correct location of Jotapata. [31]

This topic of a reconsideration of biblical Japhia is very emotive in the understanding of the location of Nazareth city of the gospels.

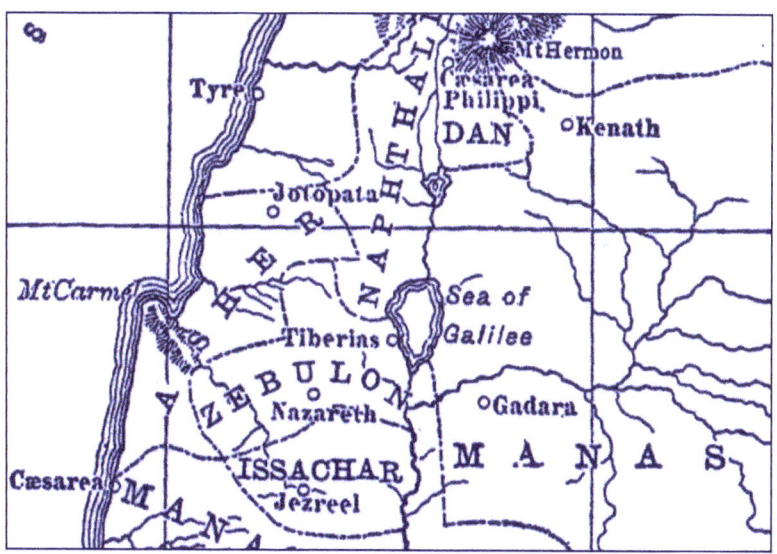

Illus. 56 Early 19th. Century KJV Bible map showing Zebulun extending to the Sea of Galilee. This was accepted until Robinson's endorsement of Japhia in 1841.

---

30 Email sent by Yigal Levin (Israeli Archaeologist and Bible Geographer) to the author on 19 February 2016. There are also other Israeli scholars who do not accept the nomination based on the topography such as Zacharia Kallai (historian/geographer), Nadav Na'aman (historian/archaeologist), Zvi Gal (archaeologist) and Ze'ev Safrai (historian/geographer). Christian scholars who have not accepted the nomination are Martin Noth (historian), Carl Keil (Bible scholar), Robert Boling (Bible scholar) and Robert Hubbard (Professor Biblical Literature).

31 Harris, T op. cit., pp. 137-152. Explains the relationship of Japhia and Jotapata based on Josephus.

APPENDIX D: A CATHOLIC SOURCE FOR NAZARETH SITES

Illus. 57 Byzantine Church at Ephesus in Turkey. Built over the proposed early 'House of Mary'. Discovered due to a vision by Anne Emmerich.

In the Roman Catholic tradition there are certain historic people with claims to a prophetic gift. One of the most popular is Saint Francis of Assisi. However there is another controversial person known as Anne Emmerich (1774-1824), an Augustinian nun who lived in Germany. Under the Catholic system of testing she has the status of venerable showing her moral credentials and acknowledgement that her gift was from God. The following are quotes from her revelations concerning some of the sites listed in this booklet.[32]

1. Nazareth walled city with gates
Jesus with some disciples walking towards the city: "they approached by the side whose gate opens to the east on the road leading to the Sea of Galilee, but they went not into the city. Nazareth had five gates" (Vol.1. p. 364-365).

2. House of Mary and Joseph
Dwelling provided by mother Anne: "The little house at Nazareth which Anne fitted up for Mary and Joseph, belonged to Anne. From her own dwelling, she could, unnoticed, reach it in about half an hour by a cross path (Vol. 1. p. 190).

Mary's house in a hamlet: "Mary's house stood on a hill outside the city, part of it extending into the hill like a cave. The top of the house however, arose above the hill, on the opposite side of which lay other dwellings" (Vol. 1. p. 372).

The place of the Annunciation: Description of Mary's room as a prayer oratory for devotion and a sleeping area at the rear. The oratory section was where "the angelic Annunciation took place" (Vol. 1. p. 191).

Mother Anne and a servant present at the incarnation event: "Some time elapsed, and then Anne and the other woman entered Mary's room, but when they beheld her in ecstasy they withdrew" (Vol. 1. p. 195).

3. Joseph's home workshop
Joseph's shed near his house (NV2): "I saw St. Joseph, out of long strips of bark – yellow, brown and green – platting [sic] screens, large surfaces, and

---

32 Schmoger, C (ed.) 2004, *The Life of Jesus Christ*, Vol. 1-4, Tan Books and Publishers Inc., Rockford, Illinois, USA. (www.tanbooks.com) used with permission.

covers for ceilings. He had a stock of his woven board-like work piled under a shed near the house" (Vol. 1. p. 289).

4. Joseph's public workshop
Joseph's workshop NC3: "Outside the city walls, where Joseph had his carpenter's shop, lived several people, poor but good, who had been known to Joseph, and among whose sons were some of the playmates of Jesus' childhood" (Vol. 1. p. 372).

5. Joseph's first burial
The burial of Joseph: "… he was wrapped from the head to foot in a white winding sheet, laid in a narrow casket, and placed in a beautiful tomb, the gift of a good man … Joseph's remains were afterward removed by Christians to Bethlehem, and interred" (Vol. 1. p. 330).

6. The Nazareth Synagogue
The synagogue was located within the city walls: "The synagogue was in the western part of Nazareth" (Vol. 2. p. 236).

7. The Execution Site
The distance to the site of 1.2 kilometre (1300 yards): "A little less than a quarter of an hour's distance from the city, rose the mountain from whose steep summit they hurled people, and whence, at a later period, they wanted to cast Jesus" (Vol. 1. p. 365).

8. The Transfiguration on Mount Tabor
The sacred caves of the prophets on Mount Tabor: "On the southeastern side of Thabor lay a cave with a garden in front. There the prophet Malachias had often sojourned. Farther up the mountain were another cave and garden where Elias and his disciples sometimes lived retired, as upon Carmel. These caves were now held as shrines by pious Jews, and thither they used to go to pray" (Vol. 2. p. 453).

The grotto of the transfiguration (T1): "Then Jesus withdrew with them into a deep grotto behind a rock which formed, as it were, a door to the cave. It was like the grotto on the Mount of Olives, to which Jesus so often retires to pray, and from it a descent led down into a vault" (Vol. 3. p. 296).

9. Mount Sarid as a spiritual site
The Prophet's Seat on Mt. Precipice / Kedumim used by Jesus for teaching: "An instruction had been announced for the following day, which was to be delivered on a height southwest of Thabor … The spot upon which Jesus taught was a beautiful plateau where, from the stone chair, the Prophets of bygone days had taught. From it one could see across the valley of Esdrelon and into the country around Mageddo (Vol. 3. p. 137).

(Esdrelon is the Jezreel valley and Mageddo is Megiddo).

APPENDIX E: PROPHETIC SIGNPOSTS OF THE MESSIAH

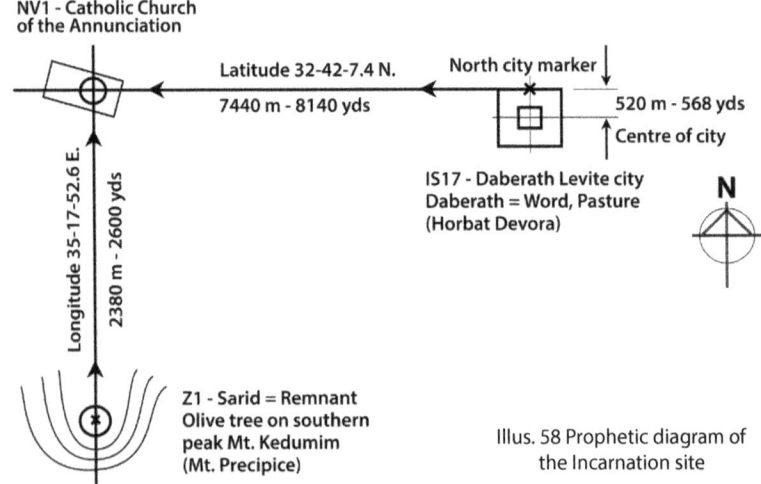

Illus. 58 Prophetic diagram of the Incarnation site

If Jesus was the Messiah and the subject of many prophecies as claimed by Christians, it would be interesting to see if there are any clues in the location of some of the events in his life. The site considered in this booklet involved the proposed place of the incarnation. Two sites can be described as prophetic signposts and the clue is found in the Hebrew root meanings in the names.

1. **Mount Sarid Z1:** This prophetic site shares the same longitude as the Church of the Annunciation. This was illustrated in No. 3. The Mount of the surviving 'remnant' aligning north with the future residence of Joseph and Mary. A pointing to the coming of the Messiah.

2. **Daberath IS17:** This Levite city near Mt. Tabor, can have several Hebrew root meanings with the definite article (Joshua 19:12). These include "The Pasture" or "The Word".

It was indicated previously that the original city of Daberath was located at a site known today as Horbat Devora just north-west of Mount Tabor near modern Deburiya that preserves the name. Levite cities had boundary markers one thousand cubits (Numbers 35:3-5, 445 metres, 486 yards) from the city walls. In the case of Daberath this location comes close to the latitude of the Church of the Annunciation if the walls were 75 metres from the centre.

The apostle John linked Jesus as the Messiah with his statement: "In the beginning was *the Word*, and *the Word* was with God, and *the Word* was God (John 1:1) [italics added]. This Levite city which can have a meaning of "The Word" had a dedicated marker where priests would have worshipped. Part of their worship on occasions could be praying for the coming of the Messiah. Eventually this was to occur 7,440 metres (8,140 yards) to the west.

REFERENCE SECTION
GLOSSARY

Bir
Arabic for a water well
Byzantine era
325–678 AD Christian empire of the East ruled from Constantinople.
Crusader era
1099–1291 AD The rule by European powers in Palestine.
Desposyni
Judeo-Christians who were blood relative descendants of the mother and father of the Virgin Mary. They would be cousins to Jesus (adelphoi in the Greek).
Early Roman Era
63 BC to 135 AD. Historical period in Palestine (includes Jesus' time).
Galilee (The)
Traditionally divided into Upper (northern Israel and southern Lebanon) and Lower (northern Israel) above the Plain of Jezreel to Beth Kerem Valley.
Hebrew Christians
There were different labels for Christians that came from a Jewish culture. They include those known as Judeo-Christians.
Hamlet
A small rural community less than 500 people in Early Roman times.
Hellenistic
332–63 BC. The Greek period begun by Alexander the Great.
Historic vs. ancient
In this book the arbitrary time frame for ancient is the BC period and historic is the AD period.
Horbat, H.
Hebrew for historic ruined site.

Joshua
The leader appointed by Moses to lead Israel into the Promised Land.
Kefar, Kefr, Kfr.
Hebrew for village.
Khirbet, Kh.
Arabic word for historic ruin.
Mishnah
Jewish period of writing 200 AD.
Moses
(1571–1451 BC) Leader of the Israelites in the Exodus. Traditional author of the Pentateuch.
Palestine
The Roman name for Israel commencing its time of rule 67 BC.
Pharisees
Jewish sect of the Early Roman era in Palestine. Known for their many rules for living.
Prophetic
Information pointing to a future event. For Christians a pointing to an aspect of Jesus the Messiah. (Rev. 19:10).
Spiritual
The non-material realm. The Bible explains three realms: the true God, the angelic creatures (godly or evil) and the human spirit. An aspect of the sacred related to a site or event.
Talmud(s)
Jewish writings (Babylonian and Jerusalem) 200 to 400 AD.
Tel, (Hebrew) Tell (Arabic)
A hill or mound often with ancient layers of human settlement.
Torah
The Jewish Law as recorded in the first five books of the Hebrew Bible.

ALPHA-NUMERIC SITE CODES

The border sites of Zebulun
Z1 – Sarid is Mt. Kedumim (Mt. Precipice) peak (geographic feature) *
Z2 – Maralah at Tel Shadud (Zebulun city No. 1)
Z3 – Dabbasheth at Tel Shammam (Zebulun city No. 2)
Z4 – Jokneam at Tel Qashish (Zebulun Levite city No. 3)
Z5 – Chisloth Tabor at Khirbet Umm al Ghanan (Issachar site)
IS17 – Daberath at Horbat Devora (Issachar Levite city)
Z8 – Japhia at Horbat Binit (Zebulun city No. 4)
Z5 – Gath Hepher at Tel Gath Hepher (Zebulun city No. 5)
Z23 – Gebere (Gabara) at Tel Adami (not in Masoretic text, only in Septuagint)
Z9 – Ith Kazin at Khirbet Qadis (Zebulun city No. 6)
Z11 – Neah at Har Arbel (geographic feature)
Z15 – Dimnah/Rimmono at Khirbet Mimlakh (Zebulun Levite city No. 7)
Z12 – Hannathon at Har Kamon (geographic feature)
Z13 – Jiphthahel Valley is the Beit Kerem Valley (geographic feature)

> * Explanation of Sarid being a geographic feature. There is a total of seven Zebulun cities. Added to the five internal cities (Kattath, Nahalal, Shimron, Idalah and Bethlehem of Zebulon) makes the total of twelve cities recorded and required in Joshua 19:10-16.
> Other sites shown on maps: A28 Akko; N10 Zer of Naphtali; Z47 Ailut (Ilut) proposed as Japheph in Roman times; Z18 Sepphoris Galilee capital and Z22 Kitron (Zebulun site misnamed at Shimron).

The Nazareth hamlet sites
NV1 – Catholic Church of the Annunciation – House of Mary and Joseph
NV2 – St. Joseph's Workshop Church
NV3 – Sisters of Nazareth Convent – St. Joseph's first burial site?
NV4 – Synagogue Church (traditional site)
NV5 – Mary of Nazareth International Center – Mary's neighbour's house?
NV6 – Orthodox Church of the Annunciation (St. Gabriel)
NV7 – Mary's Well
NV8 – Historic Bathhouse
NV9 – Nazareth Village Project

The urban Nazareth sites
NC1 – Franciscan Church compound – locality for the Nazareth synagogue?
NC2 – Yafia Byzantine site – Count Joseph's church?
NC3 – Yafia Orthodox Church (historic)
NC4 – Yafia Catholic Church and school
NC5 – Yafia Melkite Church
NC6 – Nazareth spring/well
NC7 – IAA excavation in Tel Yafia (30 metres or 33 yards south of NC2)
NC8 – Nazareth execution site on the east bank of Yafia valley?

Reference section

INDEX

A
adelphoi, Gk. 32, 61
Africanus, J. historian 32
Ahaz, King 20
Ailut, (Ilut) Tel site 6, 62
Amidah, prayer 43
angel, 16, 21, 22, 35, 36, 37, 58, 61
Anne, Virgin Mary's mother 22, 32, 58
Annunciation of Mary, i, 16, 18, 21, 22– 23, 25, 26, 28, 30–32, 53, 54, 58, 60, 62
archaeology, periods 54
Atonement, religious 45, 46
Atosh, Kh. site 57

B
Bagatti, B. archaeologist 17, 42, 50, 56
Beit Kerem,(Jiphthahel) valley 4, 62
Bethlehem, of Judea 10, 29, 59
Bethlehem, of Zebulun, 62
Binit, Horbat site 11, 50, 62
Byzantine churches, 15, 24, 26, 37, 38, 50, 54, 58, 61, 62
Byzantine Era, 29, 50, 53, 61

C
Cabul/Kabul, region 4
Caesarea Maritima, 55
Capernaum, site 3, 10, 28, 48
Catholic Church, i, 16–18, 21–23, 25, 31, 39, 51–54, 60, 62
Chisloth Tabor, site 4, 18, 49, 52, 62
Church, St. George Yafa 9, 36
conspiracy of Nazareth, 8
Constantine, Emperor 37, 55
Constantinople, capital 55, 61
Count Joseph, 37, 38, 54, 62
Crusader Era, 16, 24, 29, 49, 50, 53, 54, 56, 61

D
Dabbasheth, site 4, 18, 62
Daberath, Levite city 6, 49, 51, 60, 62
Daburiya, site 49
David, King 11, 21, 35, 36, 43
Desposyni, Jesus' relatives 16, 32, 61
Dimnah, Rimmon 4, 62

E
Early Roman Era, 5, 11, 12, 13, 16, 22, 24, 28, 30, 31, 39, 53, 54
Egeria, pilgrim 24
Eleazar ben Killir, poet 54, 56
Elias, St. church 49–51,
Elijah, prophet 16, 20, 49, 51, 52, 59
Elizabeth, rel. 10, 21, 30
Emmerich, Anne nun 58
Eth Kazin, site 4, 62
Epiphanius, historian 37
execution site, 10, 18, 44–48, 59, 62

F
Francis, St. of Assisi 24, 58
Franciscans, Catholic 14, 15, 23, 24, 26, 33, 37, 42, 48, 62
Franciscan Church, Yafia 4, 9, 13, 15, 42, 62

G
Gabara, site 62
Gabriel, angel 16, 21, 22, 53
Galilean, 5, 13, 53
Galilee, region 3, 6, 11, 28, 44, 49, 58, 61, 62, 66
Gamla, site 41
Gath Hepher, Tel site 4, 62
Gentile, 3, 33, 53, 55
Gospel, Christian message and books 2, 5, 8, 12, 22, 26, 28, 32, 37, 40, 44, 45, 47, 48, 51, 65

H
hamlet, small settlement, Nazarth 5, 6, 7, 8, 10, 12, 15–17, 30, 40, 53–55, 58, 61–63, 66
Hannathon, site 4, 62
Hapizzez, Jewish priests of Nazareth 55
Ha-Shomer, hill, Ilaniya 11
Hebrew Christians, 16, 61
Hellenistic Era, 12, 54, 61
Herod Antipas, 6

I
Idalah, site 62
Ilaniya, moshav 11, 57
incarnation of Jesus, 10, 16, 18, 22, 58, 60
Iron Age Era, 54
Isaiah, prophet 3, 11, 19, 20, 41, 44, 45
Islamic Era, 54

J
Jacob, patriarch 3, 21
James the Less, cousin to Jesus 28, 31, 32
James the Greater, 11, 42, 49, 52, 54, 56
Japhia, site 4, 11, 50, 55–57, 62
Jerome, St. scholar. 16, 24, 32, 49, 54
Jerusalem, city 4, 12, 20, 43, 48
Jesus Christ, 2, 5, 8, 10, 11, 12, 15, 16, 18, 20–23, 26–30, 32–34, 37–41, 43–45, 46, 48–52, 54, 55, 58–61, 66
Jezreel, Plain of 45, 59, 61
Joachim, (Eliachim=Heli) Virgin Mary's father 22
John, apostle, Gospel writer 11, 37, 38, 42, 49, 52, 54, 56, 60
Jokneam, Levite site 4, 62

63

J

Joseph, St., (Mary's spouse) 5, 7, 8, 10–13, 16, 17, 20–22, 26, 27, 29, 30–32, 36–39, 44, 54, 58, 59, 62, 66
Josephus, historian 3–5, 11, 52, 57
Joshua, Israelite leader 3, 4, 11, 18, 50, 61, 62
Jotapata, site 57
Jubilee, Jewish festival 10
Jude, relative of Jesus 31, 32
Judea, region 10, 11, 12, 30
Judeo-Christian, 16, 17, 23, 27, 30–33, 53, 54, 55, 61

K

Kedumim, (Precipice) Mount 15, 18–20, 42, 45, 49, 54, 59, 62

L

Late Roman Era, 33, 54
Leah, Jacob's wife 19, 20
Levite priests, 49, 51, 60, 62
Loreto, Italy 24
Lower Galilee, region 3
Luke, Gospel writer 10, 21, 22, 30, 39, 44

M

Maccabees, 54
Mamluk Era, 54
Maralah, site 4, 62
Mark, Gospel writer 10
Mary of Nazareth International Center 17, 30, 31, 62
Mary, Virgin 5, 7, 8, 10–12, 16, 17, 19–25, 28, 29–32, 35, 36, 53, 54, 58, 60–62
Mary's Well, site 17, 53
Matthew, Gospel writer 3, 5, 10, 20, 26, 31, 32, 35, 40, 49
medallion, Nazareth 55
Medieval Era, 11, 18, 24, 33, 49, 54, 56
Megiddo, site 59
Melchizedek, priest 49
Melkite Church, 33, 35, 62

Messiah, Jesus Christ 3, 16, 18, 19, 20, 22, 25, 37, 43, 45, 48, 55, 60, 61
Middle Bronze Era, 54
Mishnah, Jewish 61
Moses, Israelite leader 3, 11, 49, 50, 52, 61

N

Nahalal, Levite city 62
Nahum, prophet 20, 51, 52
Naphtali, tribal 3, 4, 51, 62
Nazareth, bath-house 17, 53
Nazareth, city (urban proposed) 5, 6, 8–15, 35, 38–40, 44, 45, 47, 54, 55–58, 59, 62, 65
Nazareth, hamlet traditonal 2, 3, 5, 6, 8–11, 14, 17, 18, 21–30, 32–34, 37, 39, 53, 54, 56, 58, 59, 62, 65
Nazareth, Synagogues 14, 17, 33, 40–43, 59, 62
Nazareth Village, historic display site 53
Neah, site 4, 62
Neanderthal, ancients 18

O

Ophna, site 54
oratory, Mary's prayer 58
Orthodox Church, 36, 39, 50, 51, 52, 53, 54, 62
Orthodox St. Gabriel, 17, 53
Ottoman Era, 54, 56

P

Palestine, 24, 55, 56, 61
Passover, celebration 12
Peter, apostle 49, 52
Pharisees, sect 46, 61
Philip, apostle 11
Pilate, Pontius 2, 15
polis, Gk. city 7, 8, 12, 13, 26
Pope Benedict XVI, 18
Precipice Mt., *see* Kedumim
Priestly Course, 56

Q

Quaresmius, scholar 54

R

remnant, from the Exile 19, 20, 60
Revelation, Book of 38
Robinson, E. explorer 11, 54, 56, 57
rolling stone tomb, 29
Roman Era, 7, 11–14, 16, 27, 28, 30, 31, 33, 39, 40, 52, 53, 54, 61

S

Sabbath, rest day 16, 44–46, 61
Sarid, Mount 4, 18–20, 60
Sepphoris, site 6, 7, 12, 62
Shimron, Tel, site 6, 62
Sisters of Nazareth Convent 17, 28, 29, 62
stoning area, execution 45–46

T

Tabor, Mount 15, 49–52
Talmud, Jewish 61
Torah, Jewish Law 8, 61
Transfiguration (Jesus), 49–52, 62

W

Way of the Sea, 3
workshop St. Joseph, home 10, 17, 26, 27, 28, 36, 58, 62
workshop St. Joseph, public shopfront 10–12, 14, 22, 35, 36, 38, 39, 59, 62

Y

Yafa, *see* Yafia 11, 35, 54, 56
Yafia, 5, 8–10, 12–16, 35, 36, 38, 39, 40, 42, 45, 54–57, 62
Yodfat, Tel 57

Z

Zebedee, father James and John 11, 42, 56
Zebulun, tribal 3, 4, 18, 19, 20, 51, 57, 62
Zoker, Desposyni 33

Reference section

PROMOTION: THE NAZARETH SERIES

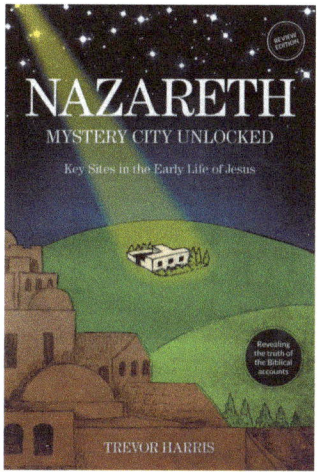

Book 1: Nazareth - Mystery City Unlocked
By Trevor Harris
Key-line Christian Research
Non-fiction/Academic/Christian
ISBN: 978-0-9925506-0-8 Print colour
Limited edition only

Nazareth – Mystery City Unlocked was a Review Edition for scholars. It reveals that the lost city of Nazareth did in fact exist if the correct definition of the city in 27 AD is explained, debunking the myth that the city never existed. The mystery of Nazareth is solved when all the facts are made clear. Also included is information on other sites of the Lower Galilee.

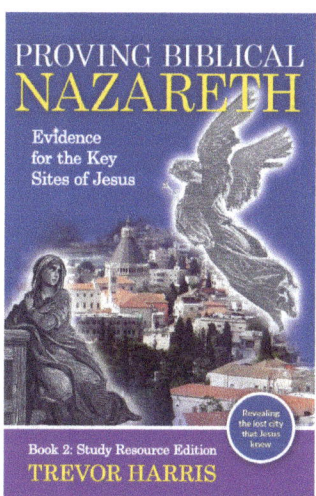

Book 2: Proving Biblical Nazareth
By Trevor Harris
Key-line Christian Research
Non-fiction/Academic/Christian
ISBN: 978-0-9925506-1-5 Print black and white
ISBN 978-0-9925506-2-2 Print colour
ISBN 978-0-9925506-3-9 ebook

This extensive resource edition provides evidence from a range of scholarly sources. Details are given for Nazareth city in the time of Jesus. It traces the story of how the urban centre became lost in time. Particular information is given on Mary and Joseph's hamlet that was part of the Jewish city. Archaeological and historical evidence is given on other sites of the Lower Galilee. Examples of prophetic site mapping are shown pointing to aspects of Jesus as the Messiah.

Key-line Christian Research upholds the reliability of the original Bible texts.
Our motto: "The Land is the fifth Gospel".
We seek to investigate Bible sites involving their history, geography and spiritual significance with passion and integrity.
We seek to publish and promote the results of our research to interested persons and groups.
Further information: Key-line Christian Research: www.biblekeylines.com